# SECRET
# SHREWSBURY

## John Shipley

AMBERLEY

John Shipley
Nov 2018

First published 2019

Amberley Publishing
The Hill, Stroud
Gloucestershire, GL5 4EP

www.amberley-books.com

Copyright © John Shipley, 2019

The right of John Shipley to be identified as the
Author of this work has been asserted in accordance
with the Copyrights, Designs and Patents Act 1988.

ISBN  978 1 4456 7845 0 (print)
ISBN  978 1 4456 7846 7 (ebook)

British Library Cataloguing in Publication Data.
A catalogue record for this book is available from the
British Library.

Origination by Amberley Publishing.
Printed in Great Britain.

# Contents

# Acknowledgements

I would like to publicly thank and acknowledge all the people, individuals and organisations that have helped with the compilation of material for this book and without whom the project could not have been completed.

Most of all to my long-suffering, proofreading wife Kate, and my son Peter Shipley for their immense contribution – rewrites, additional facts and proof checking. Plus my good friends Eric Smith and Mike Thomas for their input and Betty Smith for her photographs. The staff at Bridgnorth Public Library, and all local history groups and societies. And finally to Team Editor Jenny Stephens and all at Amberley Publishing.

I must also acknowledge the books and blogs of Shrewsbury's giant Town Crier Martin Wood; also to Shrewsbury Town Guide Maggie Love.

The material for this book has been compiled and assembled from personal research, archive material, various websites and printed matter, and of course word of mouth, all of which has been used in good faith.

Appleyards' famous delicatessen shop at the top of Wyle Cop.

View of Shrewsbury Abbey from the castle.

Whilst every effort has been made to check and recheck the facts and items in this book, if a mistake has been made myself and the publisher will seek to make amends at the first opportunity. Where possible, permission has been sought.

And lastly, please forgive me if I have not included any of your particular favourite items.

# Introduction

Welcome to *Secret Shrewsbury*. The word 'secret' traditionally describes something that one person, or no one knows. The dictionary definition is 'concealed, hidden, unseen, kept private, a mystery'. On that basis it is impossible to write about secrets, so instead I have written about some of the lesser-known aspects of Shrewsbury. Many, perhaps all, of the secrets in this book will be known by some, but hopefully they will be outnumbered by those who will not.

Every time I visit Shrewsbury I find something new to marvel at, whether it be the delightful architecture, or an aspect of Shrewsbury's history. *Secret Shrewsbury* will help the understanding of anyone interested in learning more about Shropshire's wonderful county town.

Let's begin our journey by discussing a real secret: namely exactly who first founded a settlement at Shrewsbury, and when? Unfortunately this remains an intriguing and unsolved mystery because there is so little evidence to help us. Oddly the Roman invaders of our county did not consider the site strategic or a desirable place at which to construct a defensive fortification, choosing instead a spot around 5 or so miles to the south-east at Viroconium Cornoviorum (which morphed later from Wroeken and Wroecenseter to present-day Wroxeter). At that time, the area was occupied by the Cornovii, a British tribe whose capital may have been the hill fort on the summit of the Wrekin. Around AD 50 the Romans defeated British Chief Caratacus at the Battle of Caer Caradoc (possibly near Church Stretton) to effectively end local resistance.

The current considered opinion of most experts is that Shrewsbury itself was first settled sometime between AD 520 and 594, possibly around AD 570. Viroconium appears to have been abandoned by the local indigenous Romano-British population sometime around 520, over 100 years after the Romans had left our shores. The reason would seem to be that they were driven from Viroconium by marauding Saxons.

A recent and intriguing discovery of a Neolithic presence in the Sutton area of Shrewsbury has now complicated matters. Carbon dating of a 15-inch wooden post found during an archaeological dig in the grounds of the medieval Church of the Holy Fathers of Nicaea (now owned by the Greek Orthodox Church), on what is believed to have been a Pagan burial site, tells us that the post was placed in the ground in 2033 BC. Human and animal bones, including pigs and the remains of a pregnant dog, were also found, along with medieval garment pins. Roman coins and pottery have also been discovered within the loop of the River Severn, and evidence of Bronze and Iron Age peoples have been discovered outside the loop of the River Severn at Belle Vue, Greenfields, and Berwick. There have also been late prehistoric period

Stone parish boundary marker which formally stood on the old stone bridge, demolished in 1774.

finds at Bayston Hill and Meole Brace. It's quite possible that an ancient trackway may have existed across the land within the loop of the river accessed at either end via the two fords.

In Saxon times the settlement of Shrewsbury was on two small hills with an area of marshy land plus a boggy pool in between.

## DID YOU KNOW?

The River Severn is Britain's longest river at 220 miles, and the second longest in the British Isles after the River Shannon in Ireland at 240 miles.

The Welsh name for Shrewsbury was Pengwern (Pen meaning head, end, knoll or hill, gwern meaning an Alder tree, some say Alder swamp) or Pengwern Powis, where in the seventh century it would appear resided the Celtic Prince or King of Powys, Cynddylan, who it seems was killed in AD 656 by raiding Saxons from Northumbria. Pengwern was subsequently absorbed into the Saxon Kingdom of Mercia. A 5-inch-long, eighth- or ninth-century Saxon bronze pin, now identified as a pointed stylus used for writing on wax tablets, was discovered in the late 1940s on the site of Old St Chad's Church. It has a flat edge at the end used as a kind of eraser.

A kind of census compiled sometime between the sixth and ninth centuries, known as the Tribal Hidage, lists the Wreocensate (Wrekin dwellers) peoples as one of thirty-five tribes occupying Britain below the Humber estuary; their land centres on the Wrekin, although the extent of their boundaries is not known.

The Old English name for Shrewsbury was *Scrobbesburh, or Scrobbesbyrig,* meaning either 'fort in the scrub-land region', or 'Scrobb's fort', 'Shrubstown', or 'the town of the bushes', or possibly simply named after the person who held the land, i.e. a man named Scrob. Shrewsbury's later name in Welsh is Amwythig (meaning a fortified place). Over time the name evolved to *Ciropsberie* and then to *Schrosberie,* and finally to Shrewsbury. The earliest written recording of the town is in the Charter of Wenlock Abbey dated AD 901, which refers to Scrobbesbyrig, although sadly the town didn't make it onto the list of Mercia's ten burghs. However, by AD 900 Shrewsbury had four churches: St Alkmund's, St Chad's, St Mary's, and St Juliana's (St Julian's). To further confuse matters, at various times Shrewsbury was also written as: Sloppesberie, Ciropsberie and Schrosberie. By 1086, the Domesday Book records that 'In Civitate Sciropesberie' (i.e. styled as a city) the settlement consisted of eighty-six households (eighty-two Burgesses plus four villagers), and was protected by the castle and the natural defence of the river; the tax paid was 102½ geld units.

By the Middle Ages Shrewsbury was at the centre of the wool trade; the first mention of drapers was in 1204. The Draper's Guild was incorporated by royal charter in 1462.

The name of the county developed from the name of the principle town, and so we have Scrop-scire, and Salopschire, and subsequently Schropshire. Over the centuries the name has been written in any number of other ways: Sciropscire; later as Salop and Salopia (an alternative name for both town and county). Apparently Anglo-French (Norman)

Part of the old town wall, Meadow Place.

Shrewsbury Castle Gate.

scribes found writing and pronouncing Scrobbesbyrigscir difficult and so used Sarop, then Salop, Salopsberia or Salopescira. In 1888 the county council was known as Salop County Council, but in 1980 this was changed to Shropshire County Council. Salop is not used much these days, if at all.

The question of how the name Shrewsbury should be pronounced is also a matter of some debate. Should one say it with an 'ew' as in the name of the small long-nosed rodent – shrew – or with the 'ow' as in show? I've also heard other pronunciations such as: Shroesbury, Shrewsbry, Shewsbury, Shewsbry, Shoesbry or Shrowsbury. Which is correct? You decide.

Shrewsbury, lying at the heart of a great loop in the River Severn, which almost entirely encircles the old town, was extensively developed in Tudor and Elizabethan times as the town's huge number of historic listed buildings testifies – there are more than 660, some built on Anglo-Saxon foundations. This is a town of quaint winding alleyways, passages (many known as shuts), and streets, framed by half-timbered houses, many built in the fifteenth and sixteenth centuries. The skyline of this beautiful and historic market town is crowned by a castle and a host of church spires, plus the former Benedictine monastery, i.e. Shrewsbury Abbey. There are also wonderful parks and open spaces to enjoy. It is believed that Anglo-Saxon Shrewsbury was most probably a settlement fortified by earthworks compromising a ditch and rampart, which were then shored up with a wooden stockade.

Part of the remaining wall of the infirmary of Shrewsbury Abbey.

Shrewsbury is built on two hills: St Alkmund's and St John's, not quite as dramatic as Bridgnorth's High and Low Towns, but laced with a myriad of narrow alleyways and winding streets. Centuries of historic buildings crammed in alongside each other, many leaning across alleyways, their topmost storeys almost touching. Remnants of old Town Walls, with one solitary remaining watchtower. A host of beautiful buildings and churches, with spires that seem to pierce the sky. Gorgeous views and panoramas everywhere. Climb Castle Hill from the Victorian railway station and up to the castle with its ace regimental museum on your left. Across the road on your right the statue of Charles Darwin guards the entrance to the town's library which was once the original home of the famous Shrewsbury School. Passing lovely buildings on up to High Cross. I usually arrive via the English Bridge, tackling Wyle Cop, and on along High Street, passing the Old Market Hall and Square before climbing Pride Hill to High Cross.

Few English towns have retained their medieval street plan and street names as Shropshire's county town has, although York is another fine example.

## DID YOU KNOW?

In 1719 the fifty-nine-year-old great writer Daniel Defoe described the town of Shrewsbury thus: 'This is a rich town full of gentry and yet full of trade too. It is a town of mirth and gallantry.'

# 1. A Brief History of Shrewsbury

In AD 778 the Anglo-Saxons under King Offa of Mercia took possession of Shrewsbury. In the ninth century in response to westward expansion of the Viking raiders in AD 870 King Alfred of Wessex ordered defences to be constructed around important Anglo-Saxon settlements, Scrobbes-byrig (Shrewsbury) being one of them. (NB: From now I will use the name Shrewsbury rather than the town's Anglo-Saxon name.)

During the eleventh century a London scribe wrote, 'In the year 1006 King Æthelred the Unready had gone across the Thames into Scrobbes-byrigscire to receive there his food-rent (taxes) into the Christmas season.' By then Shrewsbury was a well-established settlement. The king's representative in those days was the Scire-Reeve (Sheriff), and fortifications would have been constructed of timber walls with watchtowers at intervals all sited atop of earthen ramparts. Royal permission was granted to the town to hold a weekly market, plus an annual fair in the first three days of June. The Anglo-Saxon marketplace, roughly in the centre of the settlement, was in today's St Alkmund's Square. As a measure of Shrewsbury's important standing the town had three moneyers. These were gold and silversmiths who had permission to press silver coins using dies supplied by the royal government. Shrewsbury also had several reeves (tax collectors) who also collected fines.

The norman wall of Vaughan's Mansion in the courtyard of Shrewsbury Museum café.

## DID YOU KNOW?

In the Anglo-Saxon period marriage was taxed. A widow had to pay the king a whopping 20 shillings for a licence to remarry. Maidens had to pay 10 shillings. It was cheaper to remain single!

Shrewsbury's houses were built of timber, with wattle and daub walls, and an open fire in the centre of the room – a regular fire hazard. The fine for accidentally without negligence burning down a house was 40 shillings.

In 1066 the Norman's arrived following Duke William of Normandy's victory over Saxon King Harold at the battle of Hastings, and so began the systematic removal of Saxon nobles from their estates to be replaced by Normans. Roger de Montgomery, kinsman of the Conqueror, was given land and was created Earl of Shrewsbury. The Domesday book of 1086 lists Shrewsbury as having 250 dwellings. Earl Roger built a castle and a Benedictine abbey in this frontier town, making Shrewsbury the centre of the planned Norman suppression of the Welsh. English and Welsh Bridges were built across the River Severn. King Henry III was a frequent visitor to the town, and the Archbishop of Canterbury reputedly praised Shrewsbury (he called it Slopebury) as a town which after the bleak and barren mountains of Wales was an oasis where one could refresh oneself and recruit new staff and horses.

The Welsh weren't happy with these new Norman interlopers and constantly raided Shrewsbury, a place they still regarded as being part of Wales – remember Pengwern had once been the capital of the Princes of Powys. In 1215 Prince Llewellyn captured Shrewsbury Castle, successfully holding it for three months. As a result, new town walls were built using stone.

Shrewsbury grew steadily, spreading its environs to the districts of Frankwell, Coleham and Castle Foregate. Prosperity ensued, and the Guildhall was built. By the mid-thirteenth century the town's population had grown to around 4,000 souls. The town was granted

Shrewsbury Castle.

its charter in 1226/7, and the town's first parliamentary representative took office in 1268, the second in 1295.

Just over 100 years later the town was at the centre of a new struggle for control of the land when the Battle of Shrewsbury was fought on 21 July 1403.

The backstory to the battle began when Owain Glyn Dwr united with Marcher Lord Edmund Mortimer, 5th Earl of March, after first capturing him and demanding a ransom from the king for his release. However, the royal coffers were empty and the ransom was not paid so Mortimer switched sides, uniting with Henry Percy (Harry Hotspur), a man already miffed at the king's failure to pay his salary of office and for not paying his fair share of ransomed Scottish prisoners. Hotspur's father, the Duke of Northumberland, was also involved in his son's plot to overthrow the king. The fifteen-year-old Prince Hal (later Henry V) was at that time in Shrewsbury, and when the king heard of Hotspur's, Glyn Dwr's and Northumberland's approaching armies, fearing his son would be captured, marched with haste with an army from Burton-on-Trent to Shrewsbury.

The King marched into the town over the English Bridge, and gave orders to burn the buildings around Castle Foregate to prevent Hotspur's rebel army from reaching the castle. The rebels retreated, setting up camp on an area of common land known as 'Bolefeld', and there Hotspur waited for Glyn Dwr to come up with his Welshmen. Sadly for Hotspur the Welsh army did not arrive. Henry IV crossed the Severn at Uffington and camped near Haughmond, sending Thomas Prestbury, Abbot of Shrewsbury, and the Abbot of Haughmond to negotiate with the rebels. When talks failed, battle commenced. The fierce and bloody encounter raged on until Hotspur was shot in the face by an arrow when he inadvisedly raised his visor. On hearing the news the rebels dispersed, many running for their lives. Conflicting reports give wide variations in the sizes of the armies, and of the casualties, which were reported as being anything between 1,600 and 16,000 dead or Wounded; however it is widely accepted that Hotspur had around 14,000 men, the king slightly more. Legend has it that Glyn Dwr watched the battle from an oak tree, realising he was too late to affect the outcome. The rebel leaders were executed, with one notable exception, namely Archibald Douglas, Earl of Douglas, one of the commanders in Henry Percy's (Harry Hotspur's) rebel army.

Following the battle, rumours circulated that Harry Hotspur had not been killed and that he was very much alive. King Henry could not allow this source of possible unrest to continue and ordered Hotspur's body found. The corpse was brought to Shrewsbury's High Cross, where it was displayed propped up between two millstones, after which it was dismembered and parts of his body distributed around the country.

## DID YOU KNOW?

On the slopes of nearby Haughmond Hill there is a rocky outcrop known as Douglas' Leap, where apparently after Percy's death, the earl, whilst attempting to flee the battlefield, was thrown from his horse and was captured by the king's men. Douglas was subsequently pardoned.

*Left*: Shrewsbury's High Cross at the top of Pride Hill.

*Below*: The Church of St Mary Magdalene, Battlefield.

So great was the slaughter that the king later ordered the building of a church on the battlefield 'for the souls of those who fell'. The church is dedicated to St Mary Magdalene.

Subsequently, King Henry IV, usurper of the throne from Richard II, frustrated at failing to bring rebel Welsh prince Owain Glyn Dwr to open battle, issued a royal decree in September 1402 that 'No Welshman entirely born in Wales, having father and mother born in Wales, is allowed to purchase lands or tenements in the towns of Chester, Shrewsbury, Bridgnorth, Ludlow or any of the market towns adjoining Wales. No Welshman is to be received as citizen of burgess in any of these "burghs". Welshmen already living in such a "burgh" or being citizens or burgesses, have to find surety for good bearing towards Lord, King and the realm of England. No Welshman is to be accepted to the office of "maitre, bailiff, chamberlain or warden of gates or gaol". And no Welshman is allowed to bear armour in any of the "burghs".'

The exact site of the Battle of Shrewsbury had been disputed, and recent excavations around Battlefield Church have failed to discover any mass grave.

Shrewsbury was again at the centre of another rebellion, this time during the Wars of the Roses in 1485 when young Lancastrian heir Henry Tudor, Earl of Richmond, arrived at the town gates demanding entry. His demand placed Thomas Mytton, the town bailiff, in a bit of a dilemma. Mytton had previously sworn a solemn Oath of Allegiance to King Richard III, and to open the gates would be a serious breach of his oath, which was: 'that no enemy of the king may enter the town except over the Bailiff's body'. There followed a conscience-searching discussion between Bailiff and Burgesses about how to successfully resolve this predicament. A compromise was found, and Thomas Mytton opened the gates and lay down on the ground allowing the young earl to step over him. The oath after all had made no mention of the bailiff's body having to be dead.

The subsequent result was the Battle of Bosworth on 22 August 1485, in which Richard III was killed and Henry Tudor was declared King Henry VII, so beginning the relatively short-lived Tudor dynasty.

In 1522, King Henry VII's second son (his first, Prince Arthur had died at Ludlow aged fifteen) Henry VIII ordered Cardinal Wolsey to conduct a survey of all England, and to draw up an inventory of men between the ages of sixteen and sixty, listing their property, weapons, and possessions. The survey showed a country in decline, and Shrewsbury was no exception; the wool trade, on which the town's wealth had been built, had collapsed, and bandits terrorised the area.

With peace and unity between England and Wales, Shrewsbury's once vital importance as a frontier town was now redundant; the community was also at a low ebb. The town's walls had been allowed to crumble, and many buildings were in need of drastic repair. Among the worst was the roof of Shrewsbury Abbey, which was leaking badly. King Henry decided that change was needed, passing acts that required men, on pain of fines, to own a longbow and to practise the art of shooting it diligently. Kingsland was the place for archery practice. Owners of buildings were commanded to carry out repairs and rebuilding projects. Vagabonds and beggars were now strictly controlled. Civil disobedience was punished swiftly and severely.

The king's break with Rome in 1536 resulted in the Dissolution of the Monasteries. In Shrewsbury the abbot prevaricated, holding out against the king's order until 1540. Thomas Cromwell's soldiers eventually carried out the king's order. Much of the abbey's monastic buildings were sold off or simply destroyed; fortunately the main building survived as a parish church.

The middle of the sixteenth century saw a revival in Shrewsbury's clothing trade and therefore in the fortunes of the town. In 1552 Shrewsbury Grammar School was founded. Henry VIII's death in 1547, followed six years later by that of his Protestant son Edward VI, heralded an age of religious persecution, Catholic versus Protestant: first Catholic Queen Mary I, and then Protestant Queen Elizabeth I, who ordered the compulsory attendance of church. The working day was set at between 5 a.m. and 7/8 p.m. during the summer; in winter it was from dawn until dusk. The church of St Mary the Virgin's bells pealed out at 4 a.m., to urge the population to rise from their beds, and again at 10 p.m. in summer and 9 p.m. in winter, to signify the start of curfew.

## DID YOU KNOW?

In the 1590s Shrewsbury Clock became the proverbial standard for exactness.

In 1642, King Charles I was at nearby Wellington where he raised his standard, having first raised it at Nottingham. From Wellington he moved his flag to Shrewsbury, where he was joined by his sons, Charles and James, and cousin Prince Rupert of the Rhine. He remained in Shrewsbury until 12 October, then marched to Bridgnorth, and from there to Edge Hill for the opening battle of the Civil War.

On 9 February 1645, the Royalist garrison of Shrewsbury was surprised by a Roundhead force commanded by Sir Thomas Mytton. The town's governor, Sir Michael Earnly, was killed, and sixty gentlemen plus 200 soldiers taken prisoner. Shrewsbury was finally captured by Parliamentary forces on 23 February 1645.

In 1654, in an abortive Royalist uprising, Sir Thomas Harries made a surprise attack on Shrewsbury Castle, but his attempt failed.

## DID YOU KNOW?

The town hosts the annual Shrewsbury Flower Show, known for its floral displays, having won various awards since the turn of the twenty-first century, including Britain in Bloom in 2006. Shrewsbury Flower Show is the world's longest-running horticultural show, the first being in 1875. It is held every year, in Quarry Park, during the second week of August. The famous television gardener Percy Thrower of *Blue Peter* and *Gardeners' World* fame was Superintendent of Shrewsbury Parks for thirty years.

In the next chapter I would like to mention some of Shrewsbury's uniquely named streets, which hopefully will help to understand where places of interest are located.

The Dingle, Shrewsbury. (Courtesy of Betty Smith)

The Dingle. (Courtesy of Betty Smith)

# 2. Shrewsbury's Streets

Shrewsbury has any number of interesting streets. Here are just a few that I think are worth a mention.

## Abbey Foregate

This had a number of names. In Norman times it was called Biforegatam, then in the mid-thirteenth century it was known as Foreyeta Monachorum, in the 1500s as Abbey Foreate and East Foyryate, until the turn of the century when it became Abbey Foregate.

*Above left*: North Door, Shrewsbury Abbey.

*Above right:* Lord Hill's Doric column.

## DID YOU KNOW?

Lord Rowland Hill's Column is the world's tallest Doric column at 133 feet 6 inches. It was erected in 1816 at a cost of £6,000. The monument stands adjacent to Shire Hall, the headquarters of Shropshire County Council, a little way up the road from the hotel that bears the great man's name. Lord Rowland Hill was the Duke of Wellington's deputy, who fought in almost all the major battles of the Peninsular War, and the Battle of Waterloo.

## Bear Steps

The short flight of steps, not really a shut, opposite the top end of Grope Lane leading from Fish Street to St Alkmund's Square is named after the Bear Inn that once stood at the bottom of the steps. The surrounding buildings are part of a hall dating from around 1358/59 – the oldest in the town. Others date from then until around 1601. It was here that one of Shrewsbury's two bear pits was sited – the other was in the Quarry. There is a metal ring on the wall to which the bear would be tied before

*Above left*: Bear Steps, Fish Street, Shrewsbury. (Pen and ink by John Shipley)

*Above right*: The top of Bear Steps.

fighting in the pit. This ring was also used to lower casks of ale into the cellar of the pub. The phrase 'taking one's bearings' comes from a stranger asking to be directed to the bear pit.

## Bellstone

Bellstone is named after the large granite rock located in Morris Hall Courtyard, a remnant of the Ice Age that first captured the imagination of the young Charles Darwin, who was

Butcher Row looking towards Pride Hill.

Greyhound
Chambers,
Butcher Row.

told that this type of stone is found in Cumbria and Scotland. There was no explanation as to why it was in Shrewsbury, thus launching his curiosity and his desire to learn more about geology. The stone also marked the Bellstone parish boundary.

## Butcher Row

Butcher Row lead from St Alkmund's Place to Pride Hill. On Speed's 1610 map, Butcher Row is listed as Old Fish Street. Butcher's shops extended from and through Fish Street to High Street. This now pedestrianised thoroughfare is lined with impressive black and white timber-framed buildings. The Abbot's House stands on the corner of Butcher Row and Fish Street. (The abbot in question was the Abbot of Lilleshall Abbey who commissioned the construction, although this wasn't his residence.) The abbey rented out the upstairs accommodation to supplement their income; the ground floor was shops rented to butchers. In the 1800s there were still sixteen butchers plying their trade here; shoemakers also had shops here.

Medieval
Shopfront,
Bishop's
House, Butcher
Row.

On the opposite side of Butcher Row at the Pride Hill end is a long, three-storey, black and white timber-framed building known as Greyhound Chambers. Today part of the building is a Thai restaurant. There is a date on the building of 1392, although it is widely accepted that the building dates from the fifteenth century, probably around 1468. Its height was increased around 1611; the street-level portion was originally used as butcher's stalls. In the early twentieth century the building underwent extensive restoration, handsomely jettied at the first and second floors.

At the top end of Butcher Row is The Prince Rupert Hotel, part of which was originally Jones' Mansion, built in 1500s.

## The Dana

The Dana is in fact two very different features within the town. One is a pedestrian walkway; the other is a prison. The Dana walkway rises on the castle side of Castle Gates and continues up a flight of steps and on around the base of the castle, crossing the railway tracks via a Victorian covered footbridge, skirting the old prison before merging with Victoria Street. Flanking the original masonry bridge east of the station is a double-arch cast-iron bridge built to carry two extra platforms for the Shrewsbury to Birmingham Railway when the station was enlarged between 1899 and 1900, believed to be the only station in the country to have platforms that extend over a river. The iron sections used in the construction of the bridge were cast at Coalbrookdale.

Her Majesty's Prison in Shrewsbury, which closed in March 2013, known as the Dana, is situated across the river from the railway station, near the site of the old medieval prison. It was latterly used solely to house male prisoners, having ceased to take female convicts after 1922. There has been a prison on the site since 1793, but the present (now closed) prison building was constructed in 1877.

Platform 8 of Shrewsbury station is a now disused platform; however between 1868 and 1914 this was the main access for transporting prisoners, also used for livestock. A wall separated it from Platform 7.

The Dana Prison Gatehouse, Shrewsbury.

*Above left*: The Dana Steps.

*Above right*: Castle Gates House.

The Dana (pronounced Danner) is named after the Revd Edmund Dana (1739–1823), vicar of Wroxeter, Eaton Constantine, Harley, and Aston Botterell, all at the same time, a man with a reputation as an eccentric. Dana, who was born in Charlestown, now part of Boston, Massachusetts, was also a magistrate. He married Helen Kinnaird, daughter of Lord Kinnaird, with whom he had thirteen children; Helen was related to the powerful Vane family and also to Sir William Pulteney, owner of Shrewsbury Castle, and it was no doubt through this connection that the couple lived at Castle Gates House.

## DID YOU KNOW?

The last woman to be publicly executed in Shropshire was Ann Harris, on 16 August 1828. The last man hanged at Shrewsbury was twenty-one-year-old George Riley of Copthorne, who was executed by Albert Pierrepoint on 9 February 1961 for the murder of widow Mrs Adeline Mary Smith, aged sixty-two.

## Dogpole

In ancient times part of the old inner town wall ran across this street where there was a small low gate forcing people to duck down to pass through, thus avoiding bumping their head. The street was possibly once the original main route from Wyle Cop to the castle via the rear of St Mary's. It was also once the street where livestock was traded. Until 1824 horses were bought and sold there and after this cattle were traded until the new Smithfield opened on Raven Meadows in 1850. Before then cattle had been traded at the High Cross end of Dogpole, which became known locally as Ox Lane. In 1824 the council decided to change the name of the section of road from High Cross to St Mary's Court, to St Mary's Street. The origins of the street name are unclear, but around 1270 it was Doghepol, and in 1319 it was Doggepol. It was also once known as Dokepoll, Doke possibly deriving from Dunken (a Teutonic word meaning to dunk, duck or stoop). Poll, Pol or Pole is a medieval word meaning head or summit of a bank. Giant Town Crier Martin Wood suggests the name was Duck-hole, i.e. to duck through a small, low gate, or that because dogs were not allowed in the town in olden times, a pole had been placed here for owners to tie their pooch to. Through the years this Duck-hole or Dokepoll became Dogpole. There was once a water lane/passageway called Irkyslode which ran from Dogpole to the town walls. This was blocked by the Dominican Friars.

## DID YOU KNOW?

Shrewsbury has the world's tallest town crier, Martin Wood, who stands 7 feet 2 inches tall. Martin conducts various town tours including a ghost tour; he also writes a blog about the town.

## Fish Street

As its name suggests, Fish Street, Ffyschestrete in ancient times, was the site of Shrewsbury's old fish market, with fish stalls or fish-boards lining the street, located here from at least the 1500s, although at various times moved to St John's Hill and The Square, and back to Fish Street by 1763 where it remained until the mid-1800s. The name first appears around 1377.

## Mardol

This is a street with an unusually obscure name. Speculation of its origin has been rife and like so many other streets in Shrewsbury over the centuries, the spelling of the name has been varied: Mardeval, Mardevol, Mardefole in the 1200s. In 1596 it was Mardall, Mardwall on Speed's 1610 map, and in around 1710 it was Marowell. The first syllable of the name may derive from the Anglo-Saxon word *Maere*, meaning boundary. The second syllable may derive again from the Anglo-Saxon word for the Devil: Deofol. Therefore the whole name might mean 'Devil's Boundary'. It is anyone's guess why this should be. Centuries ago the small stream known as the Gullet Stream separated Mardol from the long-since disappeared district of Romaldsham. Sometime around the 1600s Mardol Quay was constructed on the riverside. At the bottom end of Mardol was St George's Bridge (the original Welsh Bridge). Mardol Head is simply the top of Mardol.

## DID YOU KNOW?

In medieval times Shrewsbury had a district called Romaldsham situated on the west end of the present town, centred on Barker Street, Bellstone, Hill's Lane, and St Austin's Street, and originally taking in the entire area from Shoplatch to the town walls. A gate in the town wall was named Romaldsham Postern, and allowed access to the Austin Friary. The Chapel of St Romald stood nearby. Romald was an infant Prince of Mercia, a grandson of King Penda.

## Milk Street

Located at the top of Wyle Cop where it changes to High Street, Milk street was once part of St Chad's Lane or Stury's Close Lane, and ran past Old St Chad's Church to the town walls. The town's first General Post Office was located in Milk Street.

## Murivance

The name derives from two French words – 'Mur' and 'avant', meaning before or within the walls – and referred to an open space between Belmont and St John's Hill, and from Princess Street to the town walls. Today the name Murivance applies only to a section of road along the town walls, and this only from the 1700s. There was once a postern gate here at the end of Murivance Street (now Swan Hill) which disappeared around 1743.

## Pride Hill

This wide pedestrianised street is named after the Pride family that once resided there. Roger Pride was a prominent merchant in the wool trade who owned shops and a house here during the reign of Henry III; the Pride family had died out by the time of the Tudors. However, the name first appears towards the end of the eighteenth century. The top of the street was once known as High Pavement. Pride Hill Cross is situated at the top of the hill. High Cross, also at the top, took its name from the medieval cross that once stood in the centre of the street at the top of Pride Hill. It was once a place of grisly executions and assembly. The old cross was dismantled around 1705. A market selling dairy produce and poultry once existed here when it became known as Market Cross and later as Butter Cross. At one time, one side of the street was occupied by butchers, hence Butchers' Row, also known as The Shambles. The opposite side of the street was occupied by shoemakers, hence Corvisor's or Shoemakers Row.

## Roushill
This curving street leads from Pride Hill, joining Mardol opposite Knockin Street. The name most probably derives from 'rhos', meaning a damp plain or meadow.

## Shoplatch
It would appear that the name probably derives from the name of the family Scite or Schutte that once lived here. In the Middle Ages it was known as Scheteplache. At one time Shoplatch encompassed the entire St John's Hill, extending beyond the town walls, through a gate in the wall called Shoplatch Gate, also known as Quarry Gate. Interestingly the Old English word for corner or point was sceat.

## The Slang
The Slang runs alongside the Kingsland Bridge and leads from Town Walls to the river. Over the years it has had a number of different names including Cordlone, Cordlode and Gosnell's Slang. It was once the part of Murivance that was outside the town walls.

## Thieves' Lane
This lane linked Emstry Gate with Weeping Cross. The thought is that its name came about because the road was frequently used by vagabonds who wished to avoid using the adjacent turnpike road.

Medieval buildings
at the bottom of
Wyle Cop.

## Wyle Cop

Wyle Cop is not a shut but one of the town's main access roads. The name Wyle possibly derives from 'hwylfa', which in Old Welsh simply means a road leading up a hillside. Cop derives from 'coppa', which is Welsh meaning top or head. In Saxon times the hill was much steeper; the bottom was later raised to combat the flood plain and the top was reduced in height as town grew.

### DID YOU KNOW?

Shrewsbury Town Football Club was founded in 1886, playing on its first proper ground near Racecourse Lane. In 1910 'Town' moved to Gay Meadow, on the banks of the River Severn, where famously a man in a coracle was employed to retrieve balls kicked into the river. In 2007 the club relocated to their current home, the New Meadow. The town's position near the England-Wales border has seen the club play in both the English and Welsh Cup competitions. Over the years Shrewsbury Town FC has gained a reputation as one of football's giant-killers, with stunning performances in the FA Cup against some of the league's big boys, knocking out many teams from the top divisions. The club has spent the majority of its life playing in the middle and lower divisions.

Shrewsbury Town FC have produced a number of Premier League and international players, most notably England goalkeeper Joe Hart, and Wales International Dave Edwards. Famous managers include Alan Durban, Harry Gregg, Asa Hartford, Kevin Ratcliffe, and Arthur Rowley.

# 3. Buildings and Places of Interest: The Treasures of Shrewsbury

Shrewsbury's great treasures include its historic buildings, 660 of them, many timber-framed black and white. Unfortunately there is not enough space for all of them in this book, so I'll just mention a few of my favourites.

Shrewsbury's carpenters developed a distinctive style for the construction and decoration of the timber-framed buildings that were built for the wealthy wool merchants that populated the town in the fifteenth and sixteenth centuries. The beautiful façades of many of these mansions incorporate the distinctive use of short 'S' shaped curved braces. Star shapes were also popular, along with sunken quatrefoils (circles with cusps), and carved barley-twist or cable-moulded pilasters (vertical timbers designed to give the appearance of being part of the supporting structure). Plus acanthus- (ancient Greek-) shaped carved supports beneath windows and under roof beams.

## Henry Tudor House

Situated in Barracks Passage where it adjoins Wyle Cop, this building, built around 1430–31, is reputedly where in 1485 the would-be king Henry Tudor, Earl of Richmond, stayed en route to do battle for the crown with King Richard III. It was originally a collection of shops, houses, and a brewing inn, and known also at various times as the Lion Tap, and the Trotting Horse. Nicholas Clement, a brewer and common councillor of the borough, purchased a messuage in 1429 and erected the building, jettied

Henry Tudor House, Shrewsbury.

Ornamental window, Henry Tudor House.

(overhanging) at the first- and second-floor levels, with a great hall on the first floor above the shops. Running down the side of the building is Barracks Passage, which has a wide cart entrance. It is now a popular bar and restaurant with regular live music.

## Mytton's Mansion

On Wyle Cop down the hill a bit from Henry Tudor House stands this large mansion, built in the early fifteenth century. In 1485 it was the home of Thomas Mytton, Bailiff of Shrewsbury. This is the man who lay down in front of Henry Tudor to allow the would-be king to step over his body.

No. 40 Mardol.

The King's Head, Mardol.

## The King's Head, No. 48 Mardol
The pub sign depicts a portrait of King Henry VII (Henry Tudor). One of the oldest public houses in the town, it is timber framed, black and white, with a jettied (overhanging) gallery on the upper floor, jettied also on the second floor. It is Grade II listed, three-storey, and possibly built as an inn in the late fifteenth century. King's Head Passage runs at the side of the pub. On an internal wall are the remains of a fifteenth-century wall painting representing the last supper. It is still a popular pub today.

## No. 40 Mardol
A little way towards the town on the opposite side of the street to the King's Head is another delightful building. This one isn't jettied but leans precariously towards the street. It has beautifully carved geometric patterns and ornately carved finials (vertical carved wooden features at the apex of the gables where the bargeboards meet). This black and white, timber-framed building faces another across the street, namely No. 63.

No. 63 Mardol, viewed from the top of Roushill.

Ornate carving of a dragon, on the corner of Mardol and Roushill.

## No. 63 Mardol

Currently occupied by Ellerker Opticians, this sixteenth-century building, jettied at the first and second floors, has one particularly unusual feature: the beam which is used to support the overhang was traditionally called a 'Dragon Beam' and in 1984, when the building was renovated, the original timber Dragon Beam was replaced with a steel girder; however, in the name of tradition, the local carpenter carved a wonderful upside down dragon which clings to the underside of the corner beam of the building. The carpenter was the same person responsible for the carvings on the renovated upper floor of the building on the corner of High Street and Grope Lane, which is now Costa Coffee.

## The Olde House, No. 20 Dogpole

The Olde House possibly dates from 1480. Reputedly Princess Mary Tudor (Later Queen Mary I) resided here when she stayed in Shrewsbury, a short time before moving to Ludlow Castle. There's not much in the way of evidence to support this claim apart from a painting on canvas of a pomegranate and other devices which were part of the heraldic crest of Catherine of Aragon (Princess Mary's mother) and the fact that at that time the owner of the house was Catherine's steward, Anthony Rocke. In the 1230s the Rocke family were successful in the leather and glove trade, wealthy enough that following Henry VIII's Dissolution of the Monasteries Thomas Rocke purchased 245 acres of land, twenty-eight houses, and three watermills previously owned by the abbey. The family bought the Old House and its neighbour, No. 21, the Oak House, in 1599.

The Olde House, Dogpole.

The house itself is a Grade II listed black and white timber-framed with some added brickwork with an intriguing front aspect. The façade, which was renewed sometime around 1600, disappears behind the adjacent building. The house has been altered and extended many times since it was first built. The plainly tiled roof is crowned with two superb tall chimney stacks in a triple-clustered star-shaped style, and each has a decorative capping. It has been suggested that the plot is late Saxon in origin.

## The Abbot's House, Butcher Row

The Abbot's House, built in 1458, has impressive fifteenth-century ground-floor shop windows, mostly original. These would have been covered at night with a hinged counter-board as a shutter, which was then lowered to provide a trestle-counter on which wares were displayed during the hours of trading. On the beams above the windows, meathooks can still be seen, as can latches at the top of ground-floor windows. A lovely feature is the carved Gothic-style ornamental corner post, which has been carbon dated as original. The building was built by the abbot of nearby Lilleshall Abbey.

The Abbot's House,
Butcher Row.

Medieval meat hooks, Bishop's House, Butcher Row.

Medieval latches, Bishop's House, Butcher Row.

## Ireland's Mansion

Ireland's Mansion was built *c.* 1560 or 1575 at the west end of High Street, and incorporating Nos 29, 30 and 31. This outstanding example of sixteenth-century timber-framed black and white architecture, and surely the tallest timber-framed building in the town at four storeys high (three storeys plus an attic), was built for the Ireland family (some list Robert Ireland, others name John Ireland as the first occupier), with projecting octagonal bays on the first and second floors. The family lived in the centre section with the two outer wings rented out. The uppermost floors are lit via dormer windows set into the stilted attic gables.

*Right*: Ireland's Mansion, High Street. (Pen and ink by John Shipley)

*Below*: Owen's Mansion, High Street.

## Owen's Mansion

A plaque on the front wall of Grade II listed Nos 23 and 24 High Street states that this twin-gabled with carved figurine finials building was 'Erected by Richard Owen the Elder, Gentleman. Ano Dom 1592'; however, there are claims that it was built in *c.* 1569. The building is currently occupied by The Edinburgh Woollen Mill. Timber-framed with three storeys, the second floor is jettied with a lean out of 1 in 20. The plaque on the front of the twin-gabled building immediately to the right, No. 22 High Street, one time known as Cartwright's Mansion, records a building date of 1598; however, the building itself dates from 1709, but built around an earlier structure – hence the earlier date on the plaque. This building houses the Ask Italian restaurant.

## Rowley's House, Barker Street

For all intents and purposes this complex is in fact two buildings. The rear section is a timber-framed, black and white, three-storey plus gable-dormers. Part of the building was occupied by the New Ship Inn; other parts were later used as a brewery and storage for woollen goods. The second, and later, brick building was built 1618 by wool merchant, brewer and tanner William Rowley. The building once housed the town museum before it was moved to the Old Music Hall building.

The Doorway, Rowley's House.

Timber-framed part of Rowley's House.

## The Council House Gatehouse

The Old Council House Gatehouse was built around 1620 in the Jacobean style. Passing through the archway and directly ahead is the Old Council House built in an irregular 'U' shape. The building was once used as a gaol.

Rear view of the old council offices, Council House Court.

## The Cross Keys Inn, Nos 15 and 16 High Street

This building now houses Costa Coffee, on the corner of High Street and Grope Lane. It was built in 1575 with exquisite star-shaped panelling. Oddly at one time there was another inn across the road also named The Cross Keys. In the 1990s, restoration to the upper floor of the building has seen a colourful dimension added to the carving on

Medieval building, formally the Cross Keys Inn, on the corner of Grope Lane and High Street.

the beams by the addition of the heads of Margaret Thatcher and Michael Heseltine back-to-back as they apparently were in political terms, with the words 'Poll Tax' above. In the Grope Lane section the beams have carvings of grapes and motorcycles.

## Draper's Hall

Situated in St Mary's Place, opposite the church of that name, Draper's Hall was built in two phases by Shrewsbury Drapers Company, incorporated by royal charter in 1462, starting in 1576; phase two began in 1580. The beautiful timber-framed, black and white structure has undergone sympathetic renovations over the years and still retains its earlier characteristics. Drapers, first mentioned in Shrewsbury in 1204, is a term used to describe merchants dealing in woollen cloth. The building is now used as a boutique hotel and restaurant.

As mentioned earlier, there are numerous historic buildings in the town as well as those that are timber framed, such as the following:

Draper's Hall, St Mary's Place.

## Shrewsbury Castle

Roger de Montgomery, Earl of Shrewsbury, built the first Norman timber motte-and-bailey castle on the site in 1070, on the site of an earlier Anglo-Saxon fortification to guard the open end of a loop in the River Severn – the neck of the river here is a mere 300 yards (275 metres) wide, commanding two fords in the river, which was itself a massive moat. According to reports, Earl Roger cleared out the Saxon families living beneath the castle mound and razed their homes to the ground.

King Henry II built the first red-sandstone Shrewsbury Castle in 1150–89, during a turbulent period that saw Shrewsbury under almost constant threat of siege by Welsh and English rebels. Much of the castle was demolished during the reign of King Edward I in the 1300s to allow a rebuilding and strengthening programme to take place. The castle's two drum towers were flanked by the outer wall of the great hall. The inner bailey of the castle is still intact, with lawns and flower beds; however much of what was the outer bailey has been built upon. A Norman gateway set into a curtain wall divides the two, its heavy door rebuilt by Charles I during the English Civil War; evidence of the siege of 1645 can be seen from the scars of Roundhead musket balls.

*Above left*: Drum Tower, Shrewsbury Castle.

*Above right*: Postern Gate, Shrewsbury Castle.

Like so many other fortifications, during the 1500s the castle was allowed to fall into disrepair, although some restoration took place when Queen Elizabeth I leased the castle to local merchant Richard Onslow, who added a third storey. At the start of the English Civil War the castle was garrisoned for the king, but in February 1645 it was captured by a Parliamentarian force under Colonel Mytton. However in 1660 the castle was surrendered to the Crown following the restoration of King Charles II. In 1663, the king granted the castle to Sir Francis Newport of High Ercall.

In the late eighteenth century a young Thomas Telford was commissioned by William Pulteney, 1st Earl of Bath, Whig Member of Parliament for Shrewsbury, and reputedly the wealthiest commoner in England at the time, to convert the castle into a private residence. Telford's remodelling included the folly known as Laura's Tower (c. 1790), built

Laura's Tower,
Shrewsbury Castle.

The Shropshire Regimental Museum, Shrewsbury Castle.

on the site of Earl Roger's original motte-and-bailey, as a place for Pulteney's daughter Laura (originally Henrietta Laura Johnstone) to paint and do her needlework. Sir William was so impressed with Telford's work that he persuaded the corporation to create a new post for the young man, Surveyor of Public Works for the County of Shropshire, thus beginning Telford's rise to fame. Laura's Tower is open to the public in September each year during Shrewsbury's Heritage Days.

William Pulteney is the holder of a disputed record: he was the shortest-serving prime minister of England ever, having served in office for two days (he failed to form a viable government). Actually the office of prime minister didn't officially exist until much later – Pulteney would have been known as the First Lord of the Treasury; however you won't find his name in the records. His real name was William Johnstone, and he took the ancestral name Pulteney when he inherited the Pulteney estates.

In 1924, the castle was purchased by the Shropshire Horticultural Society who then benevolently gave it to the town. The Corporation of Shrewsbury undertook a process of restoration and opened the castle to the public in 1926. Shrewsbury Castle now houses the Shropshire Regimental Museum.

Just outside the castle gate stands Castle Gates House and a little further up Castle Street stands the former Presbyterian Church of St Nicholas, built by the Victorians in the Norman style; it is now a café.

Castle Gates House.

Shrewsbury's Library, formerly the original Shrewsbury School building.

Opposite Shrewsbury Castle is a delightful building that today houses Shrewsbury's Public Library but was once the original home to Shrewsbury School. Founded by King Edward VI as a boarding school for boys by royal charter in 1552, Shrewsbury School moved to its present campus in Kingsland on the south bank of the River Severn in 1882, and is now an independent co-educational school. Ex-pupils are known as Old Salopians, and include such notables as Elizabethan poet and statesman Sir Philip Sydney, naturalist and father of today's views on evolution Charles Darwin (1809–82), broadcaster and DJ John Peel (1939–2004), author Nevil Shute (1899–1960) and Monty Python and world traveller Michael Palin CBE (b. 1943).

## DID YOU KNOW?

In Castle Street on the corner of School Gardens there is a wall plaque identifying the site of a shop in which Mr Pailin once made his original Shrewsbury Cakes. An 1840 poem includes the line, 'Oh, Pailin! Prince of cake-compounders! The mouth liquefies at thy very name.' Mr Pailin allegedly made his cakes here around 1760, although no record shows this. The product name was used by Thomas Plimmer & Sons of Castle Street, and then Phillip's Stores Ltd, who manufactured and marketed the product as 'Pailin's Original Shrewsbury Cakes'. Sadly production ceased in the Second World War due to a shortage of ingredients. Shrewsbury Cakes are really a kind of shortbread biscuit, described as being sweet and buttery, crisp and brittle to the bite, with a lovely texture. They are flavoured with caraway seeds, nutmeg, lemon and sherry. Shrewsbury Cakes probably originate from the 1500s or possibly earlier. The recipe gets a mention in a 1658 cookbook, and is mentioned in a 1700 play by William Congreve.

## Town Walls

Shrewsbury's perimeter town walls were constructed during the early part of the thirteenth century (1220–42) with grants from King Henry III, as part of the town's defences against the constant threat of marauding Welsh princes. A good section of the original wall can be found running alongside the street that bears its name, Town Walls, and in Meadow Place. Interestingly there is a section of the wall's foundation in the undercroft beneath McDonalds' fast food restaurant (now closed) in Pride Hill. This can be viewed from the Raven Meadows car park. Another section can be found in the garden of No. 18 Wyle Cop (the Illuminate Christian Bookshop). This piece of the wall has three Civil War loopholes. However, other existing sections of the walls are not obvious or easy to spot.

Situated on Town Walls is Wingfield's Tower (National Trust), the last surviving watchtower, again built in the thirteenth century during the reign of King Henry III. The building was later leased out to various people by the Town Corporation, and much later,

*Above left*: Town walls, Shrewsbury.

*Above right*: Wingfield's Tower, the last remaining watchtower.

in the 1860s, was converted and used as a residence for the coachman of John Humphries of Swan Hill Court. It was his daughter who, in 1930, bequeathed the tower to the National Trust. The tower is open six days a year. The Burghley Map of 1575 shows the town walls, with several towers, almost fully encircling the town. 'Montgomery's Tower' is today the name of a JD Wetherspoon's pub on the site of what was believed to be another of Shrewsbury's watchtowers.

'Murage' was a tax levied on citizens for the upkeep, strengthening and repair of the town's defensive walls.

## St Mary's Water Gate

Situated at the lower/river end of St Mary's Water Lane, this gate is also known as Traitor's Gate. There is a story that early on the morning of 22 March 1645 during the siege of the town by Parliamentary forces from Wem in the English Civil War, a young traitorous Parliamentary supporter, believed to have been Thomas Turner, son of a staunch Royalist barrister, and some to have been Captain John Benbow, opened this gate to allow Roundhead soldiers to enter and subsequently capture the town.

St Mary's, Water Lane, also known as Traitor's Gate.

## The Old Market Hall

Situated in the Market Square opposite the Old Music Hall, this wonderful building was built of Grinshill stone in 1596 by the Guild of Drapers to replace an earlier timber structure dating back to the 1260s. The open ground floor once housed the corn market at street level. Set into the inside wall is a tally stone with fifty holes bored into it. This was used to record and calculate the numbers and prices of transactions, a type of Tudor calculator. The upper level is supported on Tuscan columns and was where wool trading took place. The Draper's Company used the first-floor hall to negotiate prices with Welsh cloth dealers, and to hold their flannel market there each Thursday. Today on the upper floor there is a cinema and a café. Between 1870 and 1995 the magistrates' court held sessions there. Restoration of the building took place in 2000–04. Above the arch at the south-east side is a time-worn ancient statue believed to be of either Richard Duke of York (father of Kings Edward IV and Richard III) or of Edward the Black Prince (son of King Edward III). The statue once graced the old Gatehouse on St George's Bridge (sited 60 metres downstream from the site of the present Welsh Bridge at the end of Mardol) and was moved here when the bridge was demolished in 1791; there is a plaque to the left of the statue that tells all. To the right of the statue is the '3 Loggerheads' emblem of Shrewsbury and Shropshire. Below the statue a blue plaque gives the names of bailiffs serving during construction of the building: 'William Jones and Thomas Charlton, Gent,'

The Old Market Hall, The Square, Shrewsbury.

Tally Stone, Old Market Hall.

flanked by 3 Loggerheads on the right, and the arms of the Beaufort and Tudor families on the left. The coat of arms of Queen Elizabeth I, depicting the Tudor dragon and the English lion surmounted by two Tudor roses is on the south side of the building. On the south-west wall opposite the Old Music Hall is a sundial, and in the centre recessed between two windows is an angel holding a shield bearing the royal coat of arms.

## The Square

In the mid-sixteenth century, when the growth of commerce proved too great for the marketplace in St Alkmund's Square, the town bailiffs decided to establish a new and much larger town marketplace in the area known today as The Square, where the Old Market Hall stands today, but of course that building wasn't built until around 1596. The chosen area for the market was at that time a kettle-hole pool, thought to have been at least 29 feet (8.8 metres) deep, and marshy bog (a natural water-filled hollow fringed with peat bogs). Its name was Gumbestolesmore: 'Gumble' as in ducking, 'stole' as in stool, and 'more' as in marsh – hence Ducking-stool marsh. This was a place of punishment by water, a place where ducking took place. It was here that the ducking or cucking stool or gumstol or gumble stool, sometimes called the 'Stool of Repentance', was situated, at least from 1292. The stool was used for ducking the perpetrators of minor offences against society such as scolds (wives or women who nagged too much), or as punishment for dishonest traders and other offenders, including drenching defrauding bankers and brewers. Ducking was very much seen as a form of public entertainment. The Saxon's also used this method of punishment, when this instrument of torture was known to them as a scalfing-stole or 'scalding stole' (scalding stool). The ducking stool later was moved to St John's Hill. The ducking stool was also one of the instruments used to determine the guilt

Queen Elizabeth I's coat of arms, Old Market Hall.

of any person accused of being a heretic or of being involved in witchcraft. The offender was brought to a pool or river and firmly strapped to a chair-like apparatus suspended on a sort of axle so that it always stayed upright. This in turn was attached to a long sturdy wooden beam mounted on a see-saw-type of arrangement. Sometimes two beams were fixed in parallel. Some ducking stools were mounted on wheels to enable them to be easily wheeled to the water's edge, and others were hung from bridges.

It is not certain when this kind of device was last used; some records suggest 1807 or 1808. In earlier times the Catholic church placed the practice of witchcraft on the same level as heresy, citing that in effect it was the same as worshipping the Devil or false gods. As a result, anyone accused of being a witch could look forward to being subjected to all manner of painful degradation. The rise of Calvinism resulted in an increase in the number of accusations of witchcraft. Puritans appeared to revel in the spectacle of witch trials and of the resultant treatment metered out on the victims of the pointed finger. The sixteenth and seventeenth centuries saw no respite for poor old women who lived alone and who owned a black cat – two notoriously accurate symptoms of being a witch. But of course, the accusers didn't just pick on old women for their persecution; in fact anyone, male or female, was considered to be fair game by these God-fearing accusers, as long as their victims met the desired criteria. It was not just the common people who held these beliefs. King James I, himself a Calvinist, firmly believed in the existence of witchcraft, and in 1604, an Act of Parliament was passed that made the practice of witchcraft an offence. A group of Charlatans developed, known as Witchmongers, who professed an ability to identify witches. The Act was repealed in 1752 following the drowning of a woman in Tring, Hertfordshire.

The Square has been known by a number of different names through the centuries, such as Apud Pilloriam in the thirteenth century from the fact that the town's pillory stood here. Gumbestolesmore was also known as the Bishop's Pool as the area was incorporated into the estates of Robert, Bishop of Bangor.

Gumbestolestrete was the medieval name for High Street. It extended to the top of Wyle Cop. The name appears to disappear after the fourteenth century.

The ambitious new marketplace project saw the filling in of the kettle-hole to create a relatively flat area for the market. Landfill was quite possibly taken from the sloping land on the opposite side of Haystrete, today's High Street, which itself was paved in 1269–70. Records indicate that there appears to have been a marketplace of some sort here before 1261; historic documents list a number of selds (stalls) there.

A wooden-framed Guildhall (Boothall) was built on part of the site in medieval times. This was knocked down in 1783/85 and replaced by a new Shirehall around where the eyesore Princess House stands today. In 1832 Thomas Telford was commissioned to investigate the subsidence affecting the Shirehall. Test pits were dug which revealed the startling fact that much of the building's foundation had been built on oak and beech planking, and worse, at one corner the building had no foundation whatsoever. When the building was rebuilt in 1834–37, the underlying soil was replaced with 10 feet of concrete. The architect for this work was Sir Robert Smirke. The Shirehall was demolished in 1971, but was unfortunately replaced by the building mentioned earlier, a structure that many, me included, believe to be a travesty of planning. Princess House surely blights the landscape on what is otherwise a wonderful town square, flanked by fine timber-framed and brick buildings that were once

Statue of Robert Clive (Clive of India), Shrewsbury.

Medieval building, formerly The Plough Inn. The upper section is a Victorian addition.

the houses of rich and important members of Shrewsbury society. Further evidence of the boggy ground in the area has been discovered during excavations for other buildings and extensions, and bones of various wild and domestic animals such as wild boar, oxen and deer have been found. The statue of Robert Clive (Clive of India) in the square was built on a raft of concrete to prevent it sinking.

## DID YOU KNOW?

Shrewsbury Corporation accounts for 1669 list the purchase of a new ducking stool for the punishment of scolds, and in 1710/11 a payment of 6*d* was made for 'ye carriage of ye Gumble Stoole from St John's Hill to ye lower end of Mardol'.

## Newport House

Located in a prime position at the top of Dogpole is the impressive red-brick Newport House, built between 1696 and 1700 by Francis, Lord Newport, First Earl of Bradford (that's Bradford, Shropshire, not the one in Yorkshire). But first he had to dismantle, move and re-erect the timber-framed house (now called Castle Gates House) that stood on the site. Castle Gates House now stands not far from the entrance to Shrewsbury Castle; it was re-erected there in 1702, and was reputedly the residence of the earl's mistress.

Ornate Georgian rainwater gutter in The Square.

I heard a story that from the house's prominent vantage point the earl liked to observe all the people coming up the street. Newport House (the earl's family name was Newport) later became the Guildhall and housed the offices of the borough council.

The main entrance porch is Greek Doric in style and is of cast iron erected in the early 1800s. In 1838 the house was owned by ironmaster William Hazledine.

# 4. Religious Buildings of Shrewsbury

Shrewsbury's skyline is dominated by its church spires, a fact recorded so eloquently by A. E. Housman in his epic work 'A Shropshire Lad':

> High the vanes of Shrewsbury gleam
> Islanded in Severn stream;
> The bridges from the steepled crest
> Cross the water east and west.

At the top of the list of Shrewsbury's most iconic religious houses must be the Benedictine abbey of St Peter and St Paul.

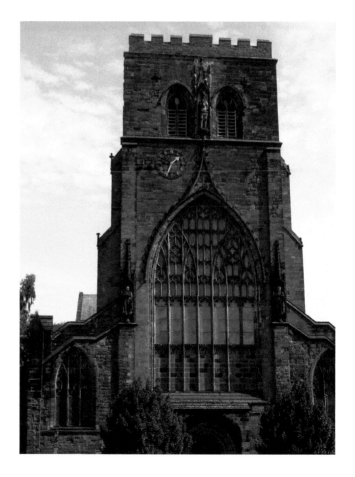

The Abbey of St Peter and St Paul, Shrewsbury.

## Shrewsbury Abbey

The Benedictine abbey dedicated to St Peter and St Paul was founded in 1083 by Roger de Montgomery, 1st Earl of Shrewsbury, and is considered to be the oldest building still standing in Shrewsbury. The abbey started life modestly as a small wooden Saxon chapel dedicated to St Peter, whose priest, councillor and chaplain, Odelerius, on returning from a pilgrimage to Rome, persuaded Earl Roger to transform the church into an abbey. Roger agreed and sent for two monks from Normandy to direct the abbey's construction. When completed the new building became the centre of Norman power in the region. Three days before his death in 1094 Earl Roger took vows as a monk. He was buried in the nave.

Benedictine monks populated the abbey for 457 years, flourishing during the early twelfth century. However the abbot, Abbot Herbert, decided the abbey needed a few religious relics, and so sent Prior Robert Pennant to Wales to find something suitable. Pennant returned in 1138 with the bones of St Gwenfrewi (St Winefride or St Winifred), a seventh-century Welsh martyr. The relics enshrined, Shrewsbury Abbey became a major centre of pilgrimage.

King Edward I called a parliament in 1283 which is believed to have met in the Chapter House of the abbey, and in Parliament Barn at Acton Burnell Castle; it was the

Refectory pulpit,
Shrewsbury Abbey.
(Pen and ink by John
Shipley)

Wilfred Owen Memorial, Shrewsbury Abbey.

first parliament to include commoners. Edward was in need of funds to support his campaign to subjugate the Welsh. He also wanted to impeach Prince Dafyd Llewellyn of Gwynedd who had recently been captured and handed over to the English authorities. The Welshman subsequently became the first person of royal blood to be executed by the grisly method of being hanged, drawn, and quartered. The execution took place at the High Cross, at the top of Pride Hill.

Henry VIII's Dissolution of the Monasteries changed much of the abbey and its buildings. In 1540 the shortened nave was left intact to serve as the parish church. Today Shrewsbury Abbey stands on a large, harp-shaped green, surrounded by trees and gravestones. The fourteenth-century west tower, with its large decorated stained-glass window, includes a statue of King Edward II. The remains of four of the huge drum-shaped columns from the original Norman church can still be seen, together with fragments of St Winifred's shrine. The east end of the nave was reconstructed in 1886/87.

The abbey was further rent asunder by non other than legendary engineer Thomas Telford, who decimated various structures during his project to widen the Holyhead Road (A5); he died before the project was completed. The remains of the fourteenth-century refectory pulpit can be found adjacent to the public car park on the opposite side of the road.

The First World War memorial below the abbey tower includes the name of war poet Lieutenant W. E. S. Owen, MC (Wilfred Owen) killed in action in 1918.

The abbey is of course the fictional home of TV's medieval monk sleuth brother *Cadfael*, based on the books of Ellis Peters (one of the pen names of famed Shropshire authoress Edith Pargeter).

Separate to the abbey Shrewsbury once had three monasteries: the Dominican Friary (Blackfriars), established between 1230 and 1232, under the slope of the abbot's

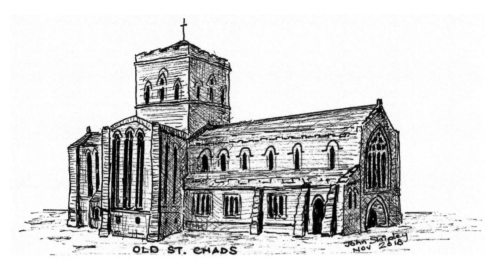

Artist's impression of Old St Chad's Church before the collapse in 1788. (Pen and ink by John Shipley)

vineyard on St Mary's Water Lane, with a private gate in the town walls; the Austin Friary (Augustinian), established 1254/55, at the lower end of Claremont Bank, with a private gate in the town walls known as Romaldsham Postern Gate; and the Franciscan Friary (Greyfriars), built 1245, also with a private gate in the town walls. All three were dissolved by Henry VIII in 1538.

## Old St Chad's Church

The exact origins of this 160-foot-long red-sandstone church are unknown. The belief is that a church was founded here during the eighth century. (Tradition has it that it may have been founded by King Offa of Mercia around AD 780.) There is a thought that it may have been built on the site of a palace of the princes of Powis which was burnt down in the Saxon wars; however, archaeological evidence for this is in short supply. St Chad was the first Bishop of Mercia in the early seventh century. An archaeological dig of the site in 1889 revealed evidence of ancient graves and Saxon structures.

This large thirteenth-century cruciform collegiate church, with a central tower over the crossing, certainly saw its fair share of disasters. In 1393 part of the old church burnt down together with a large part of Wyle Cop. The name of the man responsible for this calamity was workman John Plomer, who apparently whilst mending leads on the church carelessly left the fire in his brazier unattended. The blaze set the church roof alight, which then grew out of control, spreading to neighbouring houses. Seeing the result of his negligence Plomer ran off, calling only at his home to grab some cash, before legging it. Unfortunately for him, as he attempted to cross the River Severn at the old ford near the Stone (English) Bridge he drowned.

Almost 400 years later the tower of Old St Chad's Church collapsed shortly after the chimes of the clock struck four on the morning of 9 July 1788. Vibrations set of by the chiming caused the squat tower to shake violently. Towards the end of the eighteenth century the church had been allowed to fall into disrepair and early that summer the north-west pier of the tower had begun to show several fissures. As these cracks grew larger and with increasing speed, the persons occupying pews in the adjoining gallery became so alarmed and concerned for their safety that they stopped attending Divine services. Churchwardens were so alarmed that they called upon young Scottish engineer Thomas Telford, recently employed as County Surveyor of Public Works by Shrewsbury MP William Pulteney, to survey the building and report his findings. Telford's opinion was that the condition of the building was dangerous, chiefly caused by the needless digging of graves in ground adjoining the north-west pillar beneath the tower. He observed that the main support of the steeple had shrunk and in consequence the entire north-west side of the nave was in a dangerous state, worsened by the decay of roof timers. He stated that the whole thing could come down at any moment without much warning. He therefore advised that a dismantling and rebuilding programme be acted upon without delay. A subsequent meeting decided to ignore Telford's recommendations in favour of employing a local stonemason who claimed that by cutting away the lower portion of the tower and underpinning this with stone he could fix the problem without shoring up the structure. Sadly he was wrong, and Telford was right. On the second evening after the stonemason's men had commenced their work, the sexton entered the belfry to ring a knell prior to a funeral. He saw pieces of mortar covering the floor, and when he began to raise the great bell the tower shook and a shower of stones fell amid a cloud of dust. Greatly alarmed, the sexton grabbed the service books and whatever else of value he could carry and got out of the building. The following morning, dark and rainy, as the chimes struck four, the north, west and east sides of the tower fell onto the roofs of the nave and transept with a tremendous crash. The collapse was witnessed by only three people: a man walking by the river on the Frankwell side saw the church disappear from his view, and two chimney sweeps working in Belmont observed the tower open up when the chimes rang out. They said the tower hung for a moment as though suspended before crashing down. The nave roof, its northern range of pillars and arches, the north wing of the transept, together with a large part of the walls, plus three sides of the tower lay in complete ruin. The south side of the tower hung in the air, its beams like skeleton ribs protruding from it dangerously. Masses of stone, lead and timber, shattered pews, statues, bells, plus the organ case and gilded pipes were strewn over the area. Reportedly a few evenings earlier local campanologists of the ringing society had a lucky escape. They had assembled in the tower waiting for one important member of the team. When he failed to arrive they decided to cancel their planned bell-ringing session. There is no doubt that if they had gone ahead, the tower would have come down on top of them. The workmen's lives were spared as they had gone to get the keys to the church from the sexton prior to commencing work.

All that remains on the site today is the c. fifteenth century, Grade II listed Lady Chapel surrounded by a disused graveyard.

Rather than rebuild the ruined church a new site was sought, and a spot on the derelict town wall was chosen. The architect was to be Scotsman George Steuart, the architect of Attingham Park. Steuart drew up a number of designs, one of which was for a circular nave.

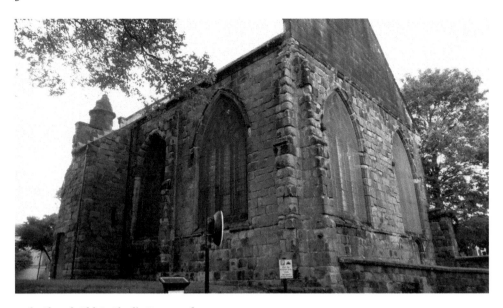

Lady Chapel, Old St Chad's Graveyard.

## DID YOU KNOW?

On 23 April 1490 King Henry VII, his Queen, Elizabeth of York, together with their first-born son, three-year-old Prince Arthur, celebrated the festival of St George in St Chad's Church.

St Chad's Church.

## St Chad's Church

The foundation stone of the new church was laid on 2 March 1790, and the church was built using white Grinshill stone in the classic elegant style on a high point overlooking Quarry Park. St Aiden's Chapel near the church entrance houses a memorial to the fallen soldiers of the 53rd Regiment of Foot, forerunner of the King's Shropshire Light Infantry (KSLI). The regimental flags of the 1st and 4th Battalions of the KSLI are housed there.

The church is the only Grade I listed circular church in the country. The tower rises to 150 feet, and the circular nave is 100 feet in diameter, which makes it the largest circular nave in Britain. Oddly, the circular shape is due to a misunderstanding (deliberate or accidental?), because the intention was to have an oblong shape, the circular design having been rejected. The new church opened 19 August 1792. Charles Darwin was baptised in the church on 15 November 1809.

Since 1987 the full title of the church is 'St Chad's with St Mary's', after St Mary's was made redundant that year.

Opposite the church is the war memorial featuring a soldier of the KSLI in khaki uniform resting on his rifle.

### DID YOU KNOW?

In the churchyard on St Chad's Terrace visitors can find the grave of Ebenezer Scrooge, a prop left behind after shooting had ended of the 1984 film version of Charles Dickens' 1843 novella *A Christmas Carol* starring George C. Scott as Ebenezer Scrooge, which was filmed on location in the town.

The interior of St Chad's Church.

War Memorial. A soldier of the KSLI leans on his rifle.

*Above left*: The gravestone of Ebenezer Scrooge, St Chad's Graveyard.

*Above right*: St Mary's Church.

## The Church of St Mary the Virgin

The current cruciform church (now redundant) began life around 1150, built on the site of an earlier stone Saxon church itself built around AD 950 and enlarged by King Edgar in 975; there are thoughts that the foundations are older. The lower red-sandstone portion of the tower dates to around 1170, and includes some stone recovered from Roman Viroconium (Wroxeter). The lighter coloured stonework and spire date from the fifteenth century, although the top of the spire came down in a gale in 1896, after which it was rebuilt along with the roof. The great Arthur Mee described the church as 'so patched outside, so beautiful within'.

St Mary's has marvellous stained-glass windows spanning six centuries, including the St Bernard window at the end of the south nave aisle, and the Jesse window at the far east end of the nave, a fourteenth-century depiction that traces the line of Jesus Christ back to Jesse of Bethlehem, the father of King David. The window was originally commissioned for the chapel of Greyfriars by the family of Sir John Charlton of Powys. Following

*Above left*: The Jesse Window, St Mary's Church.

*Above right*: The Church of St Mary The Virgin, Shrewsbury. (Pen and ink by John Shipley)

Henry VIIIs Dissolution of the Monasteries in 1538, the Jesse window was moved to Old St Chad's Church, and after that church's collapse it was relocated to St Mary's.

The fifteenth-century octagonal font is ornately carved with a floral design. Also on display are Saxon grave slabs unearthed in the nineteenth century during restoration work. The floor of the nave is of Minton floor tiles designed by Maws of Jackfield. The carved oak ceiling has carvings of birds, animals and angels.

The church sits at the heart of St Mary's Square, with its main door on St Mary's Street. The 500-year-old spire is, at 68 metres (223 feet), the third tallest in England, and provides the story of a tragedy when in 1739/40 Robert Cadman was killed. The accident occurred during the winter fair, known as 'The Great Frost of 1739'. People were skating on the frozen River Severn, and winter fun was being had by all. Shrewsbury-born steeplejack, showman, and rope-slider Robert Cadman (sometimes known as Robert Kidman) was in town to perform some of his death-defying feats. He had previously performed all over the country including St Paul's Cathedral in London, and at Dover, Derby, Newark and Lincoln. Cadman had also been employed to take down and replace the weathercock at the top of the spire, a task he had performed successfully.

A rope was attached to the spire of St Mary's and anchored in Gaye Meadow on the other side of the River Severn. Cadman signalled to slacken the rope, but his request was misinterpreted and the rope was tightened. He donned a wooden breastplate, which had a central groove, and launched himself head-first from the spire. Unfortunately the rope snapped as he was passing over St Mary's Friars and he plummeted to his death amid the spectators.

Cadman was born in 1711 and had previously performed rope stunts and feats of daring at Shrewsbury, and 1739/40 was no different. A handbill dated 24 January 1739/40 advertised his latest performance:

> This is to give notice to all lovers of art and ingenuity that the famous Robert Cadman intends to fly from off St. Mary's steeple over the River Severn on Saturday next, flying up and down, firing off two pistols, and acting several diverting tricks and trades upon the rope, which will be very diverting to the spectators.

A note was added:

> The aforesaid Robert Cadman having no one but his wife to collect what money Gentlemen and Ladies are pleased to give him, he desires the favour of those who are at a distance, either to send their servant with it, or else he intends to wait on them at their own houses.

Following the event it was later said that 'just before he set out on his mad career, he found the rope a little too tight, and he gave a signal to slacken it; but that the persons employed, misconceiving his meaning, drew it tighter. It snapped in two as he was passing over St. Mary's Friars, and he fell amid the thousands of spectators.' It was recalled that his body 'after reaching the earth, rebounded upwards several feet, the severed rope smoking in its serpentine descent'.

It was observed that Cadman's wife, who had been passing round the hat, threw away her money in an agony of grief, and ran to him. A mock-heroic yet sympathetic poem was written by an unnamed 'J. A.', presumably an eyewitness, and published in the Gentleman's Magazine:

> Nothing could ought avail, but limbs of brass,
> when ground was iron, and the Severn glass.

Near the main door of the church there is a plaque to his memory. Robert Cadman is buried in the churchyard.

In 1894 the top of the spire broke away and fell onto the roof of the nave. Fortunately no one was injured, the damage repaired and the tower restored in 1897. An ardently religious faction claimed that the collapse was an Act of God, who apparently was greatly displeased with plans to erect a statue of Shrewsbury-born Charles Darwin outside today's town library.

Actually parts of the spire and church have fallen down more than once before, most noticeably in 1571 when a 'great wind' caused the east end of the church to fall down.

*Above left*: Ancient doorway, St Mary's Church.

*Above right*: Painted Window in St Alkmund's Church.

## St Alkmund's Church

Sitting at the heart of St Alkmund's Place, at the highest point in the town, is the church of St Alkmund. Records show that there was a Saxon market held here known as the King's Market. St Alkmund was a Northumbrian prince murdered *c.* AD 800 at Northworthy (Derby) on the orders of King Eardwulf of Northumbria.

The first church on this site was built in AD 912 by Æthelflæd (Lady of the Mercians, and daughter of King Alfred), although nothing remains of the church she founded. The 184-foot-(56-metre-) high tower and spire was built around 1475 in the Perpendicular style and rebuilt in 1793/95, the main body of the medieval church having been demolished and rebuilt in the Gothic Revival style by local architect John Carline following fears of collapse after the disaster at Old St Chad's Church in 1788. The twelve identical windows designed by Carline had cast-iron frames filled with clear glass. Three of those originals have survived and have undergone restoration; the other nine were altered in the late 1800s.

The church's magnificent East Window is a painting by Francis Eginton, famous for enamel painting on glass, for which he received a commission of £200 in 1794. Eginton produced his copied version of Guido Reni's 1642 painting of the *Assumption of the Virgin*; the original was at that time in Mannheim, Germany, but today is to be found in Munich. His final bill was 210 guineas.

There is a ghostly tale originating from the time when St Alkmund's Church was rebuilt. It concerns steeplejack Robin Archerson who had worked on the new spire's construction. The local newspaper reported that one fine day Robin was sitting in the Three Fishes pub in Fish Street when he accepted a bet of a gallon of beer that he could not climb the spire and remove the weathercock. Robin then proceeded to prove them wrong. He scaled the spire, removed the weathercock, and strode proudly back into the pub with his prize to claim his gallon of beer, which he began to neck gleefully. Everyone seemed happy until it was remembered that the weathercock needed to be returned to its position at the top of the spire. Worried that this would cost them money the lads challenged Robin with a second bet that he couldn't climb the spire a second time to replace the weathercock; the prize was to be a second gallon of ale. Of course Robin accepted the bet, and despite having almost finished his first gallon of beer he grabbed the weathercock and lurched out of the inn. Once again he scaled the spire, replacing the vane correctly. Unfortunately Robin took a fatal step backward, possibly to check the alignment, and he sadly plunged to the ground. His ghost is said to haunt the church spire and the Three Fishes public house across the road.

In 1812 new bells were hung in the tower which caused the tower to sway dangerously. These were hastily removed and made their way some distance. They were later rehung in Honolulu Cathedral.

The Three Fishes Inn, Fish Street, from the terrace of St Alkmund's.

Fish Street with St Julian's Church.

## St Julian's Church (originally St Juliana's)

Situated at the lower end of Fish Street, St Julian's is dedicated to the fourth-century virgin martyr St Juliana of Nicodemia. The base of the red-sandstone tower is of Norman origin dating from around 1200; the upper section dates from the fifteenth century. The main body of the church was rebuilt by Thomas Farnolls Pritchard in 1749/59. The church became redundant in 1976 and for a time amongst other things became a private residence. It recently opened for public worship, but not in the usual style of services, open mostly on Saturdays for active Bible study and prayer.

In the 1780s, the graveyard of St Julian's Church in Shrewsbury was the scene of a disturbing event, when a man, Mr Taur, believed to be dead, was buried. The unfortunate Mr Taur was a cook staying at the Lion Hotel in Wyle Cop, who had apparently fallen

St Julian's Church, Fish Street, with the Spire of St Alkmund's Church in the background.

down dead after a coughing fit. He was buried in the graveyard. That night, the sexton and some nearby residents heard cries and screams coming from somewhere in the graveyard but ignored them, believing the sounds were caused by the wind, or the rustling of leaves. Next day, feeling uneasy and that something might be amiss, the sexton dug up the newly buried coffin. When the coffin lid was lifted the watchers fell back in horror. The underside of the lid was scored with the marks of Mr Taur's scratches as he fought to claw himself free; his fingers were worn down to the bone. It turned out that the cook had not died but had merely fallen into a coma. Mr Taur's spirit is said to haunt the hotel, together with a whole lot of other ghosts.

There are of course many other churches and chapels in the town; however lack of space prevents their inclusion.

# 5. Shrewsbury's Shuts and Passages

People have asked me to include details of Shrewsbury's quaint shuts and passages. Some I know have admitted wandering through some of Shrewsbury's narrow shuts and passages that link street to street without realising the secrets hidden within or that they are unconsciously walking through the history of the town, or how they got their name.

So, what exactly is a shut and why is it called that? A shut is described as a narrow passage, open at both extremities, enabling the pedestrian to 'shoot' from one street to another, i.e. convenient shortcuts for pedestrians. (Revd. J. B. Blakeway, noted Shrewsbury historian, describes thus: Closing the shuts off at night by locking doors helped to keep thieves and footpads from lurking in the darkness to pounce on innocent pedestrians.) By the 1800s the name shut has given way to the more liberal use of the word passage.

The vast majority have been known by a variety of names, many denoting the name of an adjacent inn, or the surname of the owners of a shop or dwelling within them. So many have disappeared during the town's morphing into what we see today. I am indebted to the local historians who have painstakingly investigated the names and locations for without them much of that knowledge would have been consigned to the Room 101 of ignominious history. Other shuts and passages were once to be found in Shrewsbury's suburbs, but again lack of space has caused their omission.

## Bank Passage
Situated between Nos 6 and 7 High Street, this was formerly known as Twenty-Steps Shut or Passage, leading from High Street to Fish Street. In the 1800s to 1910 a bank occupied No. 6, so it would seem that is where the name comes from.

## Barracks Passage
Running between Wyle Cop and Belmont Bank (once called Back Lane), Henry Tudor House is to be found here. The name refers to the reputed existence of a barracks for soldiers that was once here. It is claimed that before the Battle of Bosworth in 1485 the soldiers of Henry Tudor, Earl of Richmond and later King Henry VII were billeted here – their ghosts have been seen! In the 1700s this shut was once known as Elisha's Shut, named after a former burgess and mayor of the town Samuel Elisha. Before becoming Barrack's Passage, it was also known for a time as Lion Tap Passage, after the inn that stood there.

## Bowdler's Passage
Another shut leading from Wyle Cop, this one to the back of Bowdler's School in Beeches Lane; however this passage is now a cul-de-sac. School Passage also leads to the back of the old school.

Barracks Passage with Henry Tudor House, Shrewsbury.

*Above left*: Caernarvon Lane.

*Above right*: Coffee House Passage.

## Caernarvon Lane
Connects Mardol to Hill's Lane. In the 1400s a man named Ludovick Caernarvon lived here.

## Coffee House Passage
This passage is named after an eighteenth-century house of entertainment that stood at its mouth. Also known as Coffee House Shut, it is to be found a little to the left of the Old Music Hall, and leads from The Square to College Hill. Take a moment near the entrance and look up at the carving on the overhead beam.

## Compasses Passage
Set between Nos 70 and 71 Wyle Cop, midway between Barracks Passage and Bowdler's Passage, this shut also leads from Wyle Cop to Belmont Bank. The name probably derives from the existence of the Compass Inn in the nineteenth century at No. 71 Wyle Cop.

Compasses Passage.

## Drayton's Passage
Running from Shoplatch to Market Street, formerly known as Eddowe's Passage, and named after Eddowe's printers who occupied the shut. The Charlton family mansion was here. The doorway at the opposite end of this shut depicts the stone heads of two Talbot dogs. This was where the Talbot Inn was located in the eighteenth century.

## Golden Cross Passage
Running from Princess Street near Old St Chad's to the High Street, this passage is named after the Golden Cross Hotel, said to be the oldest hotel in town. The passage's original name was Sextry Shut, which may possibly derive from the fact that the Sacristy (Sextry) of Old St Chad's Church stood at the end of Princess Street. The Sacristy was once connected to the church by a raised covered walkway, which was still in place in the late 1700s; the church plate and other valuables were kept here. Until the late eighteenth century the shut was apparently known as Steelyard or Stillyard or Stilliard Shut after which it became Golden Cross Passage. There is a plaque at the Princess Street end of the passage which gives additional details.

Golden Cross Passage.

## Grope Lane

Running up a slope from High Street to Fish Street is a lane that was indeed, as its name suggests, a place where ladies of the night employed their trade. Its previously last recorded, and longer, name in the sixteenth century was Gropecountlane. (Without wishing to sound too salacious or to give any offence in any way, the lane's original medieval name, named for the recreational activity that took place within its darkened interior was Grope****lane.) Until more modern times most towns and cities in England had such a place; however the Shrewsbury city fathers, like those in other towns, sought to filter the descriptive Anglo-Saxon names in the interest of decency, and thus renamed theirs Grope Lane.

Another more moral story of the origin of the name comes from its dark and narrow interior, i.e. one was forced to grope one's way along the shut.

The Costa Coffee building on the corner of Grope Lane and High Street was once the Globe Inn, which in around 1820 changed its name to the Cross Keys before going through many other name changes.

Oddly in the late eighteenth and early nineteenth centuries across the street near where Starbucks is today was another Cross Keys Inn.

Grope Lane, Shrewsbury.

## Gullet Passage

Leading from The Square to Mardol Head, near where the street becomes Shoplatch, this narrow passage was once known as Gullet Shut, apparently named after the mythical Gullet Stream which ran from the Gumbestolesmore pool down to the River Severn at a place known as the Mudholes. The name may derive from the Middle English for a stream: *golate*.

Situated at the lower end of the passage is the Hole in the Wall public house, which used to be known as the Gullet Inn, a famous hostelry which in 1620 was recorded as having its own tennis court. The inn was the meeting place of the Gullet Club.

At the head of the passage, The Square end, are the remains of gate hinges and bolt holes from the gate that was used to close off the 'shut' at night. Standing a few feet from the entrance in The Square is one of Shrewsbury's two bright-red Victorian postboxes.

*Above left*: The top of Gullet Passage, The Square.

*Above right*: One of Shrewsbury's bright red Victorian postboxes, The Square, viewed from Gullet Passage.

The Hole in the Wall,
Shoplatch.

## King's Head Passage

Situated between Nos 47 and 48 Mardol, this passage was formerly known as King's Head Shut, and runs down the side of the King's Head Inn. Long ago the Town Ditch cut across this passage, which in far-off days led from Mardol to the river at Mardol Quay, now modern-day Smithfield Road, although that road did not exist before 1850. A ruined stone watchtower once stood here that may have been part of the Old Town Wall defences.

## Music Hall Passage

Visitors to the town's museum, Tourist Information Centre, and café will walk down this passage and never know it, because it is now the entrance to these places. The passage was once a shut named Fire Office Passage because the Salop Fire Office and Fire Station were here, and where horse-drawn fire engines were parked, ready to go into action to put out a fire. Long before that the passage was the entrance to Vaughan's Mansion. In the open space café courtyard the wall of the mansion can still be seen. These days it's whitewashed, but evidence of windows and doorways are clearly visible.

## Peacock Passage

Leading from High Street to Princess Street and just along from Golden Cross Passage. The King's Head Inn once stood at one end and the Peacock Inn at the other and the shut was once known as King's Head Shut. Intriguingly the shut may also once have been known by the evocative name of Snow Shoes Shut – the origin of this name is not known.

There was once a third shut between High Street and Princess Street known as Phillip's Passage but this has long since disappeared. Over the years prior to that, the shut had a multitude of names: Dun's Shut, Seymore's Shut, Gosnell's Shut, and Scoltock's Shut, all seemingly named for whoever lived there at the time. Before it was called Phillip's Passage it was called Bell Passage, probably because the stables for the Bell Inn were to be found there.

Peacock Passage.

## Phoenix Place
Known also as Phoenix Passage, but previously known as Mason's Shut and Shakleton's Shut. Situated between Nos 52 and 53 Mardol, this shut leads from Mardol to Roushill. In the 1900s Mr Phoenix's baker's shop was here, hence the name. Evidence of the houses that were once situated within this passage can be seen in the outlines of doorways and fireplaces in the walls.

## Plough Shut
This shut ran between the Plough Inn and No. 5 The Square, and ran to Mardol Head. It was once known as The Throughway and later as Plough Shut. The part of it that led to the now closed Plough Inn still remains.

## White Horse Passage
Across the river in Frankwell not far from the Welsh Bridge, White Horse Passage leads to Mountfields. It was once known as Nettles Lane from the fact that in 1580 a glover named Roger Netelles had a property here. The White Horse Inn, now disappeared, once stood on the corner.

A couple of others: St Alkmund's Shut, really an unnamed shut leading from Dogpole to St Alkmund's Square; St Julian's Shut, again this is really an unnamed shut running alongside St Alkmund's and St Julian's churches down to the head of Wyle Cop via a flight of steps. It was once known as Old Fish Street, and has not one but two right-hand bends within its length.

Here are the names of some of Shrewsbury's long-gone shuts: Bythell's Passage; Bull's Head Shut; Burying Shut/Burying Passage; Dolbrin's Shut; Factory Shut; Spoon Passage, which was a cul-de-sac; House of Correction Shut; Newell's Shut or Turkey Shut; Owen's Passage; Owen Roberts Shut; Price's Shut; Seventy-Steps Shut, previously known as Wagon and Horses Shut and Hundred Steps Shut and before that Burley's Shut, this is the only remaining shut linking Pride Hill to Raven Meadows, and is now incorporated into the shopping centre; Sherry's Shut; Sixty-Steps Shut, also known as Budgett's Passage; St Mary's Shut, a dark and extremely narrow shut once known as Little Shut, it was the longest-covered shut in the town and led from Castle Street to St Mary's graveyard; Urwick's Shut; Walker the Barbers Shut; Barett's Shut; Horse and Jockey Shut; School Passage; Sheep's Head Shut; Ship Shut; and Warter's Shut.

In the nineteenth century a number of street names were changed for various reasons, for instance Dog Lane became Claremont Street, Back Lane became Chester Street, and Kiln and Candle Lane became Princess Street.

For a more in-depth set of descriptions please see *Shrewsbury Street Names* by John L. Hobbs. The 1982 reprint version has an appendix by L. C. Lloyd, 'The Shuts of Shrewsbury'.

There is an excellent guide pamphlet 'The Shuts: A stroll around Shrewsbury' available from the Tourist Information Centre in the Old Music Hall, priced £1.

# 6. Shrewsbury's Bridges

Today Shrewsbury has a multitude of bridges; however I am only going to concentrate on three that still exist, plus two that are no longer there:

## English Bridge

The first bridge here over the River Severn was built by the Normans, possibly using timber, which was later replaced by a stone-built structure with a number of incorporated fortifications. Speculation exists that this may have been built on the site of an earlier

English Bridge.

Saxon bridge. This became known as the Stone Bridge, and may have comprised of four or five arches, possibly six, leading from the foot of Wyle Cop to a strong stone tower, built on the easternmost pier, which also housed the prison and the East Gate, also known as the Stone Gate, with a wooden drawbridge at the easternmost end, i.e. Coleham Island, where the bridge joined onto the Monk's Bridge. The approaches to the bridge also probably had timber causeways. This ancient structure reputedly had around thirty-three houses and shops on the parapet. The drawbridge was replaced with a solid arch in 1732.

Unfortunately the bridge suffered a number of disasters. At 4 a.m. on 22 January 1545/46 the Old Stone Bridge collapsed under the force of a great flood and had to be rebuilt. There is a story that when the prison tower collapsed, with all doors and windows bolted and barred, a prisoner who was chained at the time awaiting trial fell with the tower somehow escaping injury and was subsequently pardoned and set free.

On Christmas Day 1752, those God-fearing citizens of the town that resided on the Old Stone Bridge went off to church not knowing of the catastrophe that was to befall their humble homes, for when they returned they found that their homes had disappeared. Two houses on the bridge had fallen into the River Severn below. Both houses had been supported on beams crossing the navigation arch. The ends of those beams had unfortunately decayed. This sad event became known as the 'Christmas Mishap'.

This Old Stone Bridge was dismantled in stages between 1769 and 1772 to allow the building of a new bridge. The new structure was a seven-arch stone bridge, 400 feet long with a 55-foot central arch to allow boats to pass underneath.

The current Grade II listed English Bridge over the River Severn is the third bridge on this site, this one built between 1768 and 1774 to a design by Shrewsbury-born John Gwynn; however in 1921 the bridge was deemed too steep and too narrow for the growing twentieth-century traffic and was redesigned and completely rebuilt in 1926 by Arthur W. Ward, the Borough Surveyor, using much of the old facings and stonework; despite that the project still cost around £80,000. The remodelled version was due to be officially opened in October 1927 by HRH The Prince of Wales, but unfortunately due to the sudden death of his uncle, the Marquis of Cambridge, he didn't make it, so the official ceremony never took place. However not to be denied, the corporation hit on an alternative when some time later Queen Mary was driven across the unfinished bridge in her official Daimler, so the palace was approached, and the result was a plaque stating that the bridge had been officially opened by Her Majesty Queen Mary on 13 August 1927 – ingenious or what?

## Monk's Bridge

Long ago and until the early 1700s, near the spot now occupied by the English Bridge, the River Severn forked into two channels around a spit of land known as Coleham Island (Coleham Head). The eastern channel of the river (the exact path of this channel is unclear) was spanned by what was known as the Monk's Bridge or Abbey Bridge, a 950-foot- (290-metre-) long sandstone structure of possibly eleven arches, supporting a cobbled roadway which connected the island to Abbey Foregate.

Welsh Bridge, Shrewsbury.

St George's Bridge. (Pen and ink by John Shipley)

The main Severn channel was spanned by the English Bridge, connecting the foot of Wyle Cop to Coleham Island (Coleham Head), thus there were two bridges here for over 700 years. It is estimated that the combined length of the Old Stone Bridge and Monk's Bridge was greater than 1,148 feet (350 metres).

A third bridge in this area is Coleham Bridge, which spans the Rea Brook (once known as the River Meole and the Meole Brook, a tributary of the River Severn) where it runs into the River Severn, linking Coleham Island to Old Coleham. The present bridge was built around 1770 to replace an earlier a three-arch, stone, medieval bridge.

Monk's Bridge was demolished between 1769 and 1772, and land spoil from Coleham Island was deposited into the channel on either side.

## Welsh Bridge

This five-arch, stone, 266-foot-long bridge was built by local stonemasons Carline and Tilley between 1792 and 1795; they also built De Montford Bridge. The bridge lost its tower in the mid-eighteenth century, a pointed archway with a crenellated crest, flanked by two rounded corner towers. Mounted above the gate was the stone figure of a man in armour thought to be either Richard Plantagenet, Duke of York, killed at the Battle of Wakefield, or of the Black Prince, and which was moved to the Market Hall when the first bridge (St George's Bridge) was demolished.

Artist's impression of St George's Bridge. (Pen and ink by John Shipley)

Thomas Telford advised against siting the new bridge in the place it was actually built, stating that in his opinion there was a strong risk of the foundations being scoured by the eddies of the river; however his advice was unheeded and the bridge was built. The foundations for the arch-supporting structures were laid on 12-inch oak platforms sitting on the riverbed, known as raft foundations. By 1831 the riverbed under the central arch was in danger of being washed away by the force of the river when in flood; however it was saved from collapse by the tipping of barge-fulls of huge rocks around the foundations. Telford was right. Grinshill stone was used for all dressed work. The new bridge cost around £8,000 to build.

## St George's Bridge (the earlier Welsh Bridge)

Sited around 197 feet (60 metres) downstream of where the 'new' Welsh Bridge was built, opposite the end of Mardol, this earlier six-arch, plus one dry flood arch, sandstone bridge was known as St George's Bridge due to its proximity to St George's Hospital in Frankwell. As early as 1155 there was a bridge on this site, although the origin of this bridge's construction is somewhat uncertain. However it is mentioned in various records, such as by John Leyland who in his *Itinerary* records mentions the bridge as having six stone arches, one with a wooden drawbridge, and a gatehouse at each end. One of these, at the town end of the bridge, was a great and grand crenelated tower that housed the Mardol Gate; a row of small shops sat in the centre of the bridge. A second gate, known

The Railway Bridge over the River Severn.

as the Welsh Gate or St George's Gate, stood at the Frankwell end of the bridge within a tower. Leyland described the bridge as 'the greatest, fayrest and highest'.

Traces of this old bridge, which was demolished in 1795, can be found on Frankwell Quayside. The bridge was 342 feet long and was 12 feet in breadth.

Famous artist J. M. W. Turner painted *The Old Welsh Bridge* in 1794. The new bridge can be seen under construction through the arches of the old bridge. There are many illustrations of this old bridge that can be viewed online.

Other bridges are: Castle Walk Footbridge, Kingsland Toll Bridge, Port Hill Footbridge, Greyfriars Footbridge, Railway Bridge and Frankwell Footbridge.

## DID YOU KNOW?

Ditherington Flax Mill in Spring Gardens, Shrewsbury, is the world's first skyscraper, an internationally important flax mill maltings. It is a five-storey-high, iron-framed structure built in 1797 using experimental and innovative techniques that were instrumental in changing the approach to building construction, the first in the world. There is a new visitor centre charting the pioneering history of the site.

A second iron-framed flax mill was built in the Castlefields area of Shrewsbury a few years after the one at Ditherington.

# 7. Notable People

## Richard of Shrewsbury

A little-known fact is that the unfortunate Prince Richard of Shrewsbury, Duke of York, was born in the infirmary of the Dominican Friary in Shrewsbury on 17 August 1473. Richard was the sixth child and second son of King Edward IV, and his queen, Elizabeth Woodville. He is best remembered, along with his ill-fated elder brother, Edward V, as one of the Princes in the Tower (of London), whose disappearance in 1483 became an unsolved mystery that has lasted for centuries. The queen also had another child at the friary: George Plantagenet, who died in infancy.

Prince Edward was raised in the royal castle of Ludlow under the control of his Woodville relatives, whereas the young Prince Richard was kept close to her by his mother the queen.

In May 1474, Prince Richard was created Duke of York, and in 1475 was made a Knight of the Garter, adding to his titles on 12 June 1476 when he was created Earl of Nottingham, and on 7 February 1477 when he was created Duke of Norfolk and Earl Warenne. On 15 January 1478, four-year-old Richard was married to five-year-old Anne de Mowbray, 8th Countess of Norfolk.

When on 9 April 1483 his father, King Edward IV, died suddenly, Richard's elder brother, Edward V, was proclaimed king, with Richard being named as Heir Presumptive. Edward was summoned from Ludlow Castle to London for his coronation. The queen had fled to sanctuary, taking her children, including Prince Richard, with her, when their uncle, Richard, Duke of Gloucester, and Henry Stafford, Duke of Buckingham, moved swiftly to wrest Edward from the control of the Woodvilles. Edward was lodged in the Tower of London, then a royal palace, being joined there later by his younger brother, Richard.

The Bishop of Bath and Wells, Richard Stillington, came forward, swearing that Edward IV's 1464 marriage to Elizabeth Woodville was invalid because Edward had already entered a marriage contract with Lady Eleanor Talbot – in those days this was deemed a legal marriage, resulting in all children from their union to be declared illegitimate and therefore barred from the succession, which was officially enacted on 25 June 1483. Edward IV had already fathered a number of bastard children with Elizabeth Lucy.

The next in line to the throne was Richard, Duke of Gloucester, now the only surviving brother of Edward IV. King Richard III was crowned on 6 July 1483.

As stated earlier, we do not know what happened to Richard of Shrewsbury. The last reported sighting of him and his kingly brother was in midsummer 1483, although there are disputed references to the boys later than this.

If Prince Richard of Shrewsbury and his brother were murdered, who could have been responsible and why?

Various alternative theories have been put forward. One was that Queen Elizabeth did not give up Prince Richard when she was in sanctuary, but put forward a pageboy, allowing the real Prince Richard to escape to the Continent. Might he in fact have been Perkin Warbeck, brought to England by Yorkist supporters as Prince Richard of Shrewsbury, Duke of York, to claim the throne? Then there was Lambert Simnel, another originally supposed Richard of Shrewsbury, but who was eventually claimed to be the young Edward, Earl of Warwick, son of the Duke of Clarence (brother of Edward IV and Richard III). Both these young men were at the centre of rebellions. Neither succeeded and both were discredited.

William Shakespeare, taking his information from the writings of Sir Thomas More, wrote that the dirty deed was done at the order of Richard, Duke of Gloucester, then Lord Protector of England. Of course, members of the Richard III Society and many others dispute this. Why would Richard have the boys murdered? He already had the crown and the boys had officially been declared bastards. Better perhaps to display the boys' dead bodies.

Might the culprit have been the Lancastrian usurper Henry VII, a man who's claim to the throne was tenuous to say the least? Or Henry's mother, Margaret Beaufort, a conniving parent desperate to see her son on the English throne, a ruthless, ambitious woman who conspired for years to achieve this? Another alternative is Henry Stafford, Duke of Buckingham, himself with a strong claim to the throne. One thing that would appear to be certain is that the rumours of the princes' deaths coincide with the Duke of Buckingham's rebellion, and Henry Tudor's planned invasion. Could the rumours have originated from the Buckingham camp in order to further his own agenda? We may never know.

In 1674, workmen rebuilding a stairway in the Tower of London discovered the buried bones of two children, which the then reigning monarch, King Charles II, ordered interred in Westminster Abbey – the bones are in an urn bearing the names Edward and Richard. These bones were examined in 1933, and revealed that the skeletons are incomplete and that the bones are in fact a mixture of human and animal bones.

In an earlier even more bizarre twist to this already bizarre story, in 1789, when repairs were being carried out inside St George's Chapel at Windsor, workers accidentally broke into the vault containing the remains of Edward IV and his queen, and in a second, adjoining vault the coffins of two children were discovered. They were marked as containing the remains of George, Duke of Bedford, died aged two years old, and Mary of York, died aged fourteen. Subsequent investigation revealed that these two royal children are in fact buried in a different place in the chapel, raising the question of the true identity of the persons occupying the two coffins, which we may never know unless an English monarch allows the forensic examination of the bone remains. A mystery indeed, and it all began in Shrewsbury.

## Charles Darwin

Charles Robert Darwin (1809–82), Shrewsbury's most venerated son, was born on 12 February 1809 at 'The Mount' (the house is known today as 'Darwin House'), in the Frankwell area of the town. His parents were physician Robert Darwin and Susannah

The statue of Charles Darwin outside Shrewsbury Library.

(née Wedgwood). Of Charles Darwin there is no secret; however I feel compelled to include mention of him.

Charles Darwin's maternal grandfather was the famous English pottery manufacturer Josiah Wedgwood. His paternal grandfather was the noted freethinking English physician, philosopher, scientist and poet Erasmus Darwin. Both these eminent men were members of the famous Lunar Society.

Darwin was educated at Shrewsbury School, and from there he went on to study at the Medical School at Edinburgh University, his father hoping he would become a physician. Darwin then studied at Christ's College, Cambridge.

On 5 September 1821, aged twenty-two, Charles Darwin hastily boarded a stagecoach outside the Lion Hotel on Wyle Cop, Shrewsbury, bound for London to join twenty-six-year-old aristocrat Robert Fitzroy, captain of HMS *Beagle*, as a self-financed gentleman companion and naturalist on a voyage of discovery.

The ship eventually sailed from Plymouth on 27 December 1821, on a voyage that took in the Cape Verde Islands, Brazil, Argentina, the Falklands, Tierra del Fuego, Cape Horn, Patagonia, the west coast of South America, and most famously the Galapagos Islands, also visiting Tahiti, New Zealand, Australia, Tasmania, Cocos (Keeling) Island, Mauritius, St Helena, and Ascension Island, arriving at Falmouth, where Darwin disembarked on 2 October 1836; he arrived back in Shrewsbury two days later.

For more than twenty years Darwin struggled with his theories of evolution, during which time he wrote and rewrote his thesis. Encouraged by men of science, his book *On the Origin of Species by Means of Natural Selection or the Preservation of Favoured Races in the Struggle for Life* was finally published in 1859. Darwin's theory on evolution caused an uproar, dividing the scientific community and prompting the Church of England to describe his work as heresy. However Darwin's revolutionary theory transformed the understanding of how the human species evolved; his forward-thinking book is one of the most important ever written.

Facing the castle, Charles Darwin's statue sits proudly outside the town's Lending Library, once the Royal Free Grammar School (converted in 1885), which of course the great man attended as a boy.

Shrewsbury celebrates its most famous son every February in the annual Darwin Festival.

## Geoffrey Hornblower Cock

First World War ace, Group Captain Geoffrey Hornblower Cock MC was born in Shrewsbury 7 January 1896 to parents James and Adeline Anna Cock. In December 1915 he joined the 28th Battalion of the Artists Officer's Training Corps, transferring to the Royal Flying Corps on 3 June 1916 as Temporary 2nd Lieutenant where he trained with 25 Squadron, earning his pilot's licence No. 2157 in September. He was appointed Flying Officer joining 45 Squadron RFC, who left England for France 14 October 1916. Cock's first victory came on 6 April 1917 when he shot down an Albatross D III. He was appointed Flight Commander of 'B' Flight in May 1917.

In all Lieutenant Cock was credited with thirteen confirmed aerial victories (Cock claimed nineteen), flying a two-seater Sopwith 1½ Strutter. Most of his victories came

English Bridge.

between April and July 1917. He was awarded the Military Cross on 26 July 1917. He was the last surviving pilot of the original 45 Squadron that left England to fight in France.

On 22 July 1917 whilst flying on his 97th sortie against the enemy Cock was shot down over Warneton, near the Franco-Belgian border, by Wilhelm Reinhard of *Jasta 11*, surviving but unfortunately coming down behind the German lines, crashing into a shell hole. He and his observer/rear gunner, Lieutenant Maurice Murray, were taken prisoner. Cock remained a prisoner of war until his repatriation in December 1918. He made one attempt at escape but that failed.

After the war he remained in the Royal Air Force, promoted from Flight Lieutenant to Squadron Leader on 1 January 1928, and in 1935 to Wing Commander, serving in command of No. 9 Squadron RAF at Boscombe Down. He was promoted to Group Captain on 1 November 1938, serving his country in Malta during the Second World War until his retirement in 1943.

Geoffrey Cock died 16 February 1980 in Belford, Northumberland.

## John Gwynn

Shrewsbury-born architect, town planner and civil engineer John Gwynn (1713–86) worked as a carpenter before becoming a largely self-taught architect. A founder member of the Royal Academy in 1768, Gwynn is most famous as the man who built Shrewsbury's English Bridge in 1769. A friend of Dr Samuel Johnson, Gwynn was a key figure in the introduction of the 1774 Building Act. He also built Atcham's Old Bridge in 1769–71, and in Oxford built Magdalen Bridge in 1772–90, plus that city's workhouse and the covered market. In 1781 Gwynn built the bridge over the River Severn at Worcester. John Gwynn died in Shrewsbury on 28 February 1786.

## Thomas Farnolls Pritchard

Born in Shrewsbury in 1723, architect and interior decorator Thomas Farnolls Pritchard is best known as the man who designed the world's first iron bridge. Baptised 11 May 1723 at St Julian's Church in Shrewsbury, Pritchard followed his father as a joiner before turning his hand to design, specialising in interior decoration and funerary monuments. His designs were used for the construction of St John's Church in Wolverhampton. He also carried out the rebuilding of St Julian's Church in Shrewsbury, and at Hatton Grange in Shropshire. Examples of his interior work can be seen at Croft Castle, Shipton Hall and the ballroom at Powis Castle. In later life he settled down to life as a farmer. A modified version of his design for a bridge made of iron was used to construct the famous Iron Bridge over the River Severn at Coalbrookdale. Work commenced in 1777 using cast iron forged in the factory of ironmaster John Wilkinson, the bridge opening in 1779.

Pritchard died aged fifty-four on 23 December 1777 and was buried in St Julian's churchyard in Shrewsbury. Sadly he died before his famous bridge was completed.

## John Benbow

Admiral John Benbow (1653–1702) was a British naval hero. The exact date of his birth and birthplace have been widely disputed; some believe he was born at Coton Hill, Shrewsbury, others believe Benbow was born on 10 March 1653, in Newport, Shropshire. His parents were William (a tanner) and Martha Benbow.

After attending the free school in Shrewsbury, reports suggest he was apprenticed either to a butcher or to a River Severn waterman, subsequently running away to sea, joining the Merchant Navy as master's mate on the *Rupert* at Portsmouth. On 16 June 1679 he was master of the *Nonsuch*. By 1 June 1689 Benbow was in the Royal Navy as third-lieutenant aboard the *Elizabeth*, a seventy-gun ship of the line. Promoted captain of the *York* (seventy guns) on 20 September 1689, then *Bonaventure* (fifty guns) on 26 October, and *Britannia* on 12 November. From there he was appointed Head of Chatham Dockyard, and then transferred to Deptford in March 1689/90 in the same capacity. In the summer of 1690 he was back at sea as captain of the *Sovereign*.

In 1694, Benbow's solution to French privateers who were running amok was to fill a 300-ton merchant vessel with 20,000 pounds of gunpowder, mortar bombs, iron bars, glass, bullets, chains and nails, which he sailed into the harbour at St Malo and detonated, before leading men ashore where he burned the convent. In his early naval days, Benbow also fought Algerine Barbary corsairs.

Promoted to the rank of Vice-Admiral of the Blue, Benbow achieved his greatest fame fighting the French during the War of Spanish Succession (1701–14). Benbow's seven-ship squadron had been ordered to the West Indies to seek out the French and keep Spanish possessions out of French hands. On 19 August 1702, off Cape Santa Marta, off the coast of present-day Columbia, Vice-Admiral Benbow's lookouts spotted a French squadron, giving chase for five days; however four of his captains deliberately lagged behind. Benbow's flagship HMS *Breda*, a seventy-gun, third-rate ship of the line, along with the *Ruby*, kept in touch with the French. However at daybreak on 25 August 1702, with the exception of the *Falmouth*, the rest of squadron had not closed with the enemy. Even so, Benbow decided the time was right to bring the French to battle, and without hesitation ordered his squadron to attack, sending his flagship at the enemy in a vigorous attack. However his headlong assault was not mirrored by all the other ships in his squadron. A number of captains under his command refused to support his decision to attack. Benbow was severely wounded, his leg shattered by French chain-shot; however he continued to fight until it was clear his valiant action would not be supported by his squadron. He was forced to disengage and return to Port Royal in Jamaica. The battle became known as 'Benbow's Last Fight'.

Once in port Benbow instigated courts-martial against all but one of his captains – George Walton of the *Ruby* – two of which, Richard Kirby of the *Defiance* and Cooper Wade of the *Greenwich*, were found guilty of cowardice and were sent to Plymouth where they were shot aboard HMS *Bristol* on 16 April 1703. Captain Constable of the *Windsor* was cashiered, and Thomas Hudson of the *Pendennis* died before the trial. Captains Christopher Fogg of the *Breda* and Samuel Vincent of the *Falmouth* were permitted to return to the service. Sadly John Benbow died at Port Royal in Jamaica on 4 November 1702, of fever and complications after his leg had been amputated, before they were punished. He was buried in the chancel of St Andrew's Church in Kingston, Jamaica, ensuring his place in the list of British naval heroes. The inscription on Benbow's tomb states he was fifty-two years of age when he died.

Admiral John Benbow was lionized, becoming a hugely popular figure throughout the country, and his exploits were often celebrated in song. In Robert Louis Stevenson's book *Treasure* Island, Jim Hawkins' mother's inn is The Admiral Benbow. There are also many public houses that still bear his name, including the one in Swan Hill, Shrewsbury. In Shrewsbury there is also Benbow Quay, Benbow Close and Benbow Business Park.

Members of Benbow's wider family included another John Benbow, who had been a clerk to the chancery and who had been granted arms in 1584. Also and more famously Captain John Benbow, born either 1610 or 1623 (the year of his birth is not clear), and who was probably the admiral's uncle. This John Benbow served with some distinction in the Parliamentary army as Lieutenant of Horse during the English Civil War, and was celebrated for his part in the capture of Shrewsbury in February 1645, for which he was promoted to the rank of captain. One story is that it was he who opened St Mary's Gate to let the Roundheads into the town. However, possibly following the execution of King Charles I, he became disaffected and changed sides to the Royalist cause, raising a Regiment of Horse, and joining the army of Charles Stuart (later King Charles II) at Nantwich, receiving the rank of Colonel of Horse. Benbow was captured after the Battle of Worcester in 1651, taken to Chester where he was court-martialled, found guilty of high treason, and sentenced to be 'shot to death at some convenient place in the town of Shrewsbury on Wednesday 15 of this instant, October 1651 at about one of the clock the same day'. Sentence was duly carried out on Shrewsbury Castle Green; reports say he was executed in the cabbage garden, later known as the bowling green, near the castle. Captain John Benbow's grave can be found in Old St Chad's graveyard. His body was interred on the 16th.

*Above left:* Memorial to Admiral John Benbow, St Mary's Church.

*Above right:* The gravestone of Captain John Benbow, shot by the Roundheads in 1651, Old St Chad's Graveyard.

## Benjamin Disraeli

One of Shrewsbury's more illustrious English MPs was the legendary Benjamin Disraeli (21 December 1804–9 April 1881), politician, statesman, novelist and bon viveur, who owed Shropshire a huge debt of gratitude – why? Let me tell you his story.

Disraeli was born into a Jewish-Italian family of Sephardic Jewish origin. However when he was twelve his father, Isaac D'israeli, a literary critic and historian, had him baptized a Christian, but for that foresight Disraeli would never have been able to even think of a career in politics, because of the deep-rooted anti-Semitism that existed at that time.

### DID YOU KNOW?

Until 1858 people of the Jewish faith could only stand for parliament if they took the oath of allegiance 'on the true faith of a Christian'.

Benjamin Disraeli.
(Pen and ink by
John Shipley)

At the age of eighteen Benjamin changed his name from D'israeli to Disraeli. Disraeli's early life was unnotable, his education little more than rudimentary; no public school or university for young Benjamin, despite his brothers being sent to the prestigious Winchester College. Upon leaving school his father had him articled to a firm of solicitors – Swain, Stevens, Maples, Pearse and Hunt – a profession that Disraeli had little enthusiasm for. Instead he took to gambling, and enjoyed philandering. He had affairs with many women, including Lady Henrietta Sykes.

His dress sense earned him the reputation as a bit of a dandy, and raised more than a few eyebrows. In stark contrast to the sombre style of the period, he liked to wear his hair in long black ringlets, and revelled in wearing flamboyant clothing. His shirts had lace cuffs, topped off with canary yellow waistcoats, green velvet trousers, silk stockings and shoes with silver buckles, a fop in every sense who was often to be found in fashionable London salons, arm in arm with his various mistresses, many of whom were married.

All of this gave rise to him being described as a 'tinselled coxcomb whose attire was more in keeping with that of an Italian dancing master'.

Nor was Disraeli good at business. He speculated heavily on the Stock Exchange, and in a South American mining venture which cost him dearly. In 1825, in conjunction with Scottish publisher John Murray (1778–1843), a friend of Disraeli's father, he published a daily newspaper to compete with *The Times*, *The Representative*, which failed after only six months. In 1826, he launched a novel titled *Vivian Grey*, published anonymously, ostensibly by a 'so-called man of fashion', Part 1. The book caused a sensation amongst London society, and when the true name of the author was discovered he was pilloried as a man pretending to be higher up the social scale than he was. The other three parts of the novel were published in 1827.

Following this, Disraeli suffered what might be called a nervous breakdown and spent the next three years in the country, and on the coast where his father had taken houses. In 1830, he travelled around Europe and beyond, contracting a sexually transmitted disease along the way, returning to England in 1831 when his travelling companion died.

Politics now became his passion, and 1832 saw him electioneering as a Radical in High Wycombe, failing to gain election on four separate occasions at High Wycombe and Taunton, until finally, in 1837, he was accepted as Conservative candidate for one of the two seats for Maidstone in Kent, alongside Windham Lewis, an election which he duly won. Lewis died soon after.

Life in parliament didn't go smoothly. His maiden speech was a disaster, and corruption was everywhere; there was to be no secret ballot until 1837. The Maidstone election proved to be expensive. In those days voters expected to be paid in return for the support, costs that Disraeli could not afford to pay – so he didn't!

In 1839, he married Mary Anne Lewis, the wealthy widow of Windham Lewis, a woman twelve years his senior, and her income of £5,000 a year brought some relief to the depleted Disraeli coffers, but she was kept in the dark as to the severity of his debts. His father bailed him out on at least three separate occasions.

It didn't take long for the Maidstone Conservatives and Disraeli to fall out, and they made it known that they would not wish him to be their candidate at the next election. So Disraeli had no choice but to move on. But to where? He needed a relatively safe seat, hoping for one that would not cost him too much. His friend, Lord Forrester of Wiley Hall, near Broseley, suggested he stand for Shrewsbury.

Shrewsbury at that time had a population of around 18,000 souls, and returned two Members of Parliament, and what's more both seats were vacant. However, all was not as it appeared. The town had in fact gained notoriety for being corrupt for many years. The election in 1796 had reputedly cost the successful candidate in the region of £100,000.

That said, the opportunity to stand for Shrewsbury provided Disraeli with the springboard he so desperately needed. However, he soon found himself in a bear pit of a bitter campaign where both sides accused the other of dishonest tactics. Anonymous posters appeared around town, and paid-for crowds heckled and hurled abuse at the candidates, and in many cases threw missiles such as rotten eggs and stones. Bully boys, ruffians, bargemen, colliers and factory men were hired to intimidate voters, and streams of negative articles were published by the county's newspapers. And as if this wasn't bad enough, Disraeli's earlier discrepancies came back to bite him on the bottom.

His opponents accused him of an abuse of parliamentary privilege, stating that he was both morally and politically dishonest, and that he was only standing to avoid bankruptcy and subsequent imprisonment – in those days MPs were exempt from prosecution. Broadsheets accusing him of being £20,000 in debt were tacked up all over the town, together with lists of his creditors, including tailors, hosiers, upholsterers, Jewish moneylenders, housekeepers, and anyone who had been foolish enough to put their trust in him.

Local solicitor William Yardley got the Liberal *Shrewsbury Chronicle* to publish a long condemnation, which of course Disraeli publicly denied. There is no doubt that he was spending way beyond the limit of what he could afford. Expensive clothes, an active London social life, European travel, plus the estate of Hugenden Manor, which he had purchased, all cost more than he possessed. His only income was from his writings, plus what he could borrow from his father, or from moneylenders, as MPs received no salary at that time unless they were members of the cabinet. He needed money to pay for drinks and dinners, not to mention more direct bribes, all expenses politicians were expected to fork out for.

Disraeli's response was to deny everything. He published a broadsheet of his own declaring Yardley's claims to be utterly false, accusing his opponents of an unprecedented dastardly attack on his person, full of meanness and malice. Yardley challenged Disraeli to a duel, and peace was only brought when the mayor intervened. Both men were bound over to keep the peace. However, anti-Semitism raised its head again, with Disraeli regularly regaled with shouts of Shylock, and Old Clothes. He even had bits of roast pork on sticks waved at him.

The *Salopian Journal*, who favoured the Conservative cause, came to Disraeli's defence, printing the message that: 'The friends of Mr Disraeli are satisfied that he is not in debt and that he is a man of honour.'

An attack on Liberal supporters at a meeting in Barker Street brought accusations that the Conservatives had hired bully boys from Birmingham to disrupt the meeting. The *Shrewsbury Chronicle* described the violent and chaotic scenes, the bludgeoning blows, the indiscriminate kicking of people already on the ground, the blood on the victims, the shrieks of women, and the half-dead bodies that were carried away. Relief came when polling day eventually arrived – 29 June 1841. The Conservatives won both seats with Disraeli and George Tontine duly elected Members of Parliament for Shrewsbury.

The country returned Sir Robert Peel as Prime Minister of the new Conservative government, in which Disraeli had high hopes of being asked to join as a cabinet minister. He was dining at Loton Park with Sir Baldwin Leighton when news was brought that an angry opposition mob were gathering at Frankwell to attack him upon his return to the town. Wisely Disraeli stayed at Loton for a few more days, before returning to London.

Unfortunately for him Disraeli did not get the cabinet post in Peel's government that he so desired, some Torys declaring they would not have him in the government at any price.

So, the knives were still out for him; even an election petition to unseat him and George Tontine, a frequent tactic at this time, and which had previously worked at Shrewsbury, failed because the Liberals had two of their own Gloucester MPs in the same situation. After a fraught nine months a compromise was reached and all petitions were dropped, and Disraeli and Tontine kept their seats in parliament.

Benjamin Disraeli's fortunes continued to take a turn for the better. He became leader of the Conservative Party, and ultimately Prime Minister of Great Britain on two separate occasions. He was a favourite of Queen Victoria, who, in 1876, conferred on him the title of 1st Earl of Beaconsfield, and Viscount Hughenden. Not too shabby when one considers his background.

In later life Disraeli suffered from ill health, asthma, gout and bronchitis, and before he died was almost blind. He was buried at the church of St Michael and All Angels, which stands in the grounds of Hughenden Manor. There is a memorial to him in Westminster Abbey.

When he died in 1881, the townsfolk of Shrewsbury flew flags at half-mast, and traders closed their shops, as they remembered with fondness his six years as their MP.

St Alkmund's Church and The Three Fishes Inn, Fish Street. St Julian's Church is in the background.

# About the Author

Retired managing director John Shipley has lived in Bridgnorth, Shropshire, since emigrating from the Black Country in 1968, and is now an author and artist. He and his wife, Kate, have two sons and two grandsons.

An ardent season ticket-holding fan of Wolverhampton Wanderers FC, John has had two books published about the club, plus two about Nottingham Forest, and one about Aston Villa. He is also the author of four Westerns written under the pen names of Jake Shipley and Jack Matthews. His book The Little Book of Shropshire was his first about his adopted county, followed up by three more about Shropshire: The A-Z of Curious Shropshire, Shropshire's Military Heritage, and 50 Gems of Shropshire.

Secret Shrewsbury is John's fourteenth book to be published and his fourth about Shropshire. Look out for John's next book with Amberley Publishing: 50 Gems of the Black Country, available from Amberley later in 2019.

Also by the Author:

*Writing as John Shipley:*
The Little Book of Shropshire
The A-Z of Curious Shropshire
Shropshire's Military Heritage
50 Gems of Shropshire
Wolves Against the World – European Nights 1953-1980 (Wolverhampton Wanderers)
Wolverhampton Wanderers Champions 1953/54
Nottingham Forest Champions 1977/78
Aston Villa Champions 1980/81
The Nottingham Forest Miscellany

*Writing as Jake Shipley:*
Montana Skies
Montana Vengeance
Comanche Dawn

*Writing as Jack Matthews:*
Lynching At Prospect Falls